# God Works Through Women Too:

## Lessons Learned from the Good and Bad Women of the Hebrew Bible/Old Testament

By
Helene M. Harris

# Table of Contents:

# Introduction

We all know about the men of the Hebrew Bible, but what about the women? We cannot forget the influence they had on the Jewish people. Some were good influences, some had negative influences. Nonetheless, I believe it is important to honor them. Even the women who were not Godly need to be mentioned. This book will delve into some of the most influential women in the Hebrew Bible. I decided to write this book in alphabetical order, not when the women appeared in the Bible.

# Chapter 1
## Abigail –1 Samuel 25

Abigail's story begins with her husband, Nabal. Nabal was a very wealthy. He had one thousand goats and three thousand sheep, as well as much land. However, Nabal was not of good character. In fact, he was a horrible person. Abigail was intelligent and beautiful and of good character, unlike her husband who treated people poorly. Nabal was a selfish man and in his dealings with people was not considerate or fair. His moral character was the opposite of Abigail.

David, in the meantime, was hiding from Saul who was trying to kill him. David and his troops found themselves encamped in Nabal's area. They had been in and around Nabal's property for a period. Meanwhile, David and his troops were getting low on supplies. Remember, they were on the run from Saul. David sent his some of his men to Nabal to ask for supplies. David instructed his men to inform Nabal that David had treated Nabal's servants well. David and his troops did not mistreat Nabal's servants, nor steal any sheep. Since David did not take any of Nabal's belongings, or harm his servants, he figured that Nabal would give him some food and other needed supplies. David was wrong. David sent ten of his troops to Nabal with a message from David. David told his men to tell Nabal, "Long life to you! Good health to you and your household! And good health to all that is yours. Now I hear that it is sheep-shearing time. When your shepherds were with us, we did not mistreat them and the whole time they were at Carmel nothing of theirs was missing. Ask your own servants and they will tell you. Therefore, be favorable toward my men, since we have come at festive time. Please give your servants and your son David whatever you can find for them." What David told his men to say to Nabal is that we never harmed your men or stole your sheep. Therefore, can you spare some food for us. We treated you and yours well, please help us out.

Nabal would have none of this. His reply to David's men was, "Who is this David? Who is this son of Jesse? Many servants are breaking away from their masters these days. Why should I take my bread and water and the meat I have slaughtered for my shearers and give it to men coming from who knows where?" In other words, no way!! When David's men returned and told him what Nabal said, David was incensed. Not only did Nabal refuse to give the supplies, but he also maligned David's name. David then told his men to "strap on your swords". He set out with four hundred men to kill Nabal and all the males in his household.

Thankfully, one of Nabal's servants told Abigail what had transpired. He told her that David had treated them very well. He sent greetings to Nabal and asked for some food. The servant told Abigail that Nabal was rude and hurled insults to David's men about David. The servant went on to tell Abigail that, "these men (David's men) were very good to us. They did not mistreat us, and the whole time were out in the fields near them nothing was missing. Night and day, they were a wall around us the whole time we were herding our sheep near them. Now think it over and see what you can do, because disaster is hanging over our master and his whole household." He is such a wicked man that no one can talk to him."

The quick-thinking Abigail sprang into action. She took two hundred loaves of bread, two skins of wine, five dressed sheep about sixty pounds of grain, a hundred cakes of raisins and two hundred cakes of pressed figs and loaded them on donkeys. Without telling her husband, she and her servants went to meet David. They met on a mountain ravine. David said to Abigail, "It's been useless-all my watching over this fellow's property in the wilderness so that nothing of his was missing. He has paid me back evil for good. May God deal with David, be it ever so severely, if by morning I leave alive one male of all who belong to him!"

Abigail got off her donkey and literally apologized for her husband's actions. She told David that Nabal was a wicked man and that his name means Fool. She went on tell David not to pay attention to Nabal. She also told David that when God granted him to be ruler over Israel, it would be a burden to him if he had needless bloodshed on his hands. She in other words, told him that to kill these people for no reason is wrong and would not benefit him in the future. She gave David the food she had brought. David was touched by her words and actions. He accepted the food. He then said to her, "Go home in peace. I have heard your words and granted your request."

When Abigail arrived home, Nabal was in the house hosting a banquet. He was also very drunk. She decided this was not the right time to tell him what she had done. In the morning when Nabal was sober, Abigail told him what happened between her and David. Nabal became ill with a heart condition. Ten days later the Lord struck Nabal and he died. When David heard that Nabal was dead, he thanked God for Nabal's death, but also thanked

God for preventing David from doing wrong. He then sent word to Abigail asking her to become his wife.

The story of Abigail is important. Had she not intervened; many innocent people would have died. David was going to commit mass murder. Not only did she prevent this, but she also ensured David would be the ruler of Israel without the stigma of innocent people dying at his hands because of revenge and anger.

## Lessons learned from Abigail:

Sometimes the worst situations we are in can bring out the best in us. Abigail was involved in a toxic, dysfunctional marriage. Nabal was described as "surly and mean in his dealings." Unfortunately, Nabal's household turned a blind eye, probably because they did not want any negative repercussions from Nabal. Abigail was the opposite of her husband but was caught in the middle of her morals and her marriage. When she found out how her husband treated David and his troops, she acted.

1. **Do not let fear and anxiety hold you back.** No matter how frightening or threatening a situation is, if we believe in GOD, He will be with us. GOD can use any of us for any purpose at any time. Abigail acted fast, to stop David's actions that could have resulted in needless deaths, as well as tarnishing David's name. David reacted instead of thinking the situation through. She took control of the situation and sent food to David and his troops. She could have easily done nothing. Then, alone, she went to talk to David.

She spoke to him with honor and respect. Abigail knew GOD was with her. Because of this her actions saved her household.

2. **Be humble and kind. Do not be an instigator.** Instead of the blame game, she asked for forgiveness on behalf of her household. GOD used Abigail to show David that making rash, impetuous decisions could have dire consequences. David realized that he could have killed innocent people. Abigail took a risk here because she did not know how David would react, but she did the right thing. She righted the wrong her husband did. She spoke to David and he listened.

3. **Think before you speak-**Abigail thought before she spoke. She knew what she told David could have an impact positively or negatively. She looked at the big picture and had David look at the big picture. She reminded him that GOD was on his side and that he was destined for greatness. She did not "shoot from the hip."

4. **Think about others and how your decisions/ actions will affect them-**Decisions that we make have consequences, some negative, some positive-Abigail was not thinking of herself but protecting her husband and her household. She was thinking of others before herself. By being loyal to God, she acted in a selfless manner—she put the needs of others ahead of her own. She also showed respect to David instead of denigrating him. Again, she reminded David that GOD was with him and would bless everything he did (and GOD did). After talking with David, the only thing she

asked of him is to be remembered when GOD brought him success. Abigail put the needs of others before that of herself.

5. **Trust in GOD-**GOD was with Abigail. By acting humbly, Abigail was rewarded. He gave her the strength and courage to confront David about the potential consequences of his proposed actions to kill Nabal and everyone in his household. And Abigail was rewarded. When Nabal died, David made Abigail his wife. Abigail was taken care of the rest of her life.

6. **Do good deeds, treat people with respect. Speak kind words, trust in GOD.** He will take care of us!!

(1)

# Chapter 2

## Bathsheba -2 Samuel 11&12

The story of Bathsheba evokes the question, was she a victim, complicit in committing adulty or is this a love story?

The story of Bathsheba begins in the spring when the kings go off to war. David sent Joab out with the king's men and the whole Israelite Army to destroy the Ammonites. David remained in Jerusalem. One evening David was walking around the roof of his palace. From his vantage point, he saw a woman bathing. The woman was very beautiful, and David was smitten. He sent one his servants to find out who she was. The man came back and told David that the woman was Bathsheba, the wife of Uriah the Hittite, (Uriah was with the king's men fighting the Ammonites). Still intrigued by her, David sent a messenger to fetch her. She came to David and they slept together. After having sex, Bathsheba went back to her home. A while later she found out she was pregnant. She then sent a message to David explaining her condition. David was unsure of what to do. So, he sent word to Joab to send Uriah to come to the palace to see David. When Uriah arrived at the palace, David asked him how Joab was, how the soldiers were and how the war was going. He then told Uriah to go to the home he shared with Bathsheba. Uriah was a man of integrity. He would not go home, but instead he slept at the entrance to the palace with the servants. When David found out that Uriah did not go home, he asked him why. Uriah replied to David that since the Ark is in a tent, the other soldiers are camped in open country, he did not think it was right to eat and drink and make love to Bathsheba, his wife. David's plan was for Uriah to make love to Bathsheba. That way he would think the child is his not David's. The illicit affair would be wiped away. Not so. David asked Uriah to stay one more night. He invited Uriah to eat and drink with him. Uriah got drunk and David thought for sure he would go to Bathsheba, but he did not. He slept on a mat with the servants. David must have panicked. He sent a letter to Joab that Uriah carried back instructing Joab to put Uriah out in the front where the fighting is the fiercest. Then David instructed Joab to leave Uriah there by himself without any support. He will be struck down and die. Joab obeyed King David's orders. He put Uriah in a place where the strongest battle occurred. Uriah died in battle. When David found out, he told Joab's messenger to tell Joab to press on with the fighting.

When Bathsheba found out her husband was dead, she mourned for him. After the time of mourning was over, David brought her to his house, and she became his wife. God was mad at David for having an affair with someone else's wife and then planning his (Uriah's) death. Seven days after the baby boy was born, he died. Bathsheba obviously was upset that her baby died. But since David repented, Bathsheba, became pregnant again and this time gave birth to Solomon. God chose Solomon to be the leader of Israel, succeeding his father, David.

The story of Bathsheba is interesting. She certainly cheated on her husband. Was it because David was king, and she did not or could not refuse him or was she infatuated with him? We will never know the answer to this. What we do know is she gave birth to the great King Solomon. Bathsheba has secured her place in history.

## Lessons learned from Bathsheba:

1. **We have free will to make choices-**Bathsheba's choice resulted in the death of her first child. When David sent for her, Bathsheba could have sent a message back to him that "no, I will not meet with you. I am married." The choices we make have consequences, some positive, some negative. We need to talk to God before making controversial decisions.

2. **Take time to think thing through-**Bathsheba took time to mourn the death of her husband Uriah and then the death of her son. I want to believe that during this time, she asked God for forgiveness. There will be times in our lives that we need time to heal and talk to God. Bathsheba's son Solomon wrote about a time such as this, (Ecclesiastes 3:4) – "be wise and allow yourself all the time you need to heal. "It is important that we surround ourselves with God's people and God's Word.

3. **God ultimately had a plan-**Because David repented, God gave him Solomon and other children. Look at Solomon's achievements!! Ask forgiveness for our sins—God will reward us.

(2)

# Chapter 3
## Daughters of Lot—Genesis 19

The story of Lot's daughters is one that is discrepancy between Rabbinical scholars. The city of Sodom was evil to the core. Sin was abounding and egregious. One evening two angels arrived. Lot was sitting at the entrance to the city. When Lot saw them, he bowed down to them and offered his house for the angels to spend the night. The angels at first refused, but Lot was insistent. The angels then entered Lot's home. He prepared a meal for them and they ate. Before they had gone to sleep, men from every part of the city of Sodom, both young and old surrounded Lot's house. They told Lot to bring the men out, so they could have sexual relations with them. Lot begged them not to do "this wicked thing." He had two virgin daughters who have never slept with a man that he would be willing to sacrifice in order for the angels to be left alone. Lot told the men that the men of Sodom that these two men have under protection of his roof. In other words, leave! The men of Sodom told Lot, "get out of our way". They kept bringing pressure on Lot and moved forward to break the door down. But the angels inside reached out and pulled Lot back into the house and shut the door. The men of Sodom, young and old were struck with blindness. The two angels told Lot to take his family and leave the City. God was going to destroy it. The exact number of daughters Lot is unknown but is speculated that he had two married daughters and two unmarried daughters. In Genesis 19, it is mentioned that Lot told his sons-in-law that they needed to leave the City. They scoffed at him. When dawn arrived, the angels told Lot that he needed to "Hurry! Take your wife and your two daughters out of here or you will be swept away when the city is punished." The two angels grasped the hands of Lot, his wife and two daughters and led them safely out of the city. The angels told Lot to flee towards the mountains and not to look back at the city. Lot asked the angels if he could go to Zoar instead of the mountains. They agreed but told him to hurry because they could not destroy the City until Lot and his family reached Zoar. Sodom was annihilated. Unfortunately, Lot's wife looked back at the City and was turned into a pillar of salt.

Meanwhile, Lot and his two daughters left Zoar and settled in the mountains, because he was afraid to stay in Zoar. He and his two daughters lived in a cave. One day the older daughter said to the younger, "Our father is old, and there is no man around here to give us children—as is the custom all over the earth. Let's get our father to drink wine and then sleep with him and preserve our family line through our father." That night they got their father to drink wine, and the older daughter went in and slept with him. He was not aware of it when she lay down or when she got up.

The next day the older daughter said to the younger, "Last night I slept with my father. Let's get him to drink wine again tonight, and you go in and sleep with him, so we can preserve our family line through our father." So, they got their father to drink wine that night also, and the younger daughter went in and slept with him. Again, he was not aware of it when she lay down or when she got up. So, both of Lot's daughters became pregnant by their father." Both had sons. The older daughter had a son who she named Moab, who was the father of the Moabites. The younger daughter son's name was Ben-Ammi, who was the father of the Ammonites. Both the Moabites and the Ammonites caused great problems for the Jewish people.

The Jewish Rabbinical scholars are conflicted by this story. Some think that Lot may have engaged in incest with his daughters, but this is not proven. At any rate, these two nameless daughters had sons by incest of their doing, not their father's initiation. This action created a race of people that were very much against Israel and caused much strife for the Jewish people.

## Lesson learned from Lot's daughters:

1. **We have choices-** Lot's daughters falsely believed that they were the last humans on earth. Their father, Lot, made a poor decision in leaving the town of Zoar even though he was told by angels that Zoar will not be destroyed. Instead of trusting in God's angels, he took his two daughters to live alone in a cave. Alone in the cave with their father, the daughters concluded that they are the last people alive on earth. Lot's daughters than made the decision that they must procreate. They got their father drunk and both were impregnated to save humanity. Both daughters gave birth to sons; one Moab and the other Ben-ammi. Both sons were the ancestors of the Moabites and Ammonites, both enemies of Israel. (3)
Had Lot known that other cities survived, he probably would not have made the decision to

isolate himself and his daughters. Were Lot's daughters wrong in their decision to commit incest with their father for the sake of future generations? Both sons were ancestors of peoples who were enemies of Israel. So, it did not turn out so good for Lot's daughters.

# Chapter 4

## Deborah—Judges 4

The story of Deborah is intriguing and reminds us that women too have a place in leadership. Deborah was the only female judge in Israel.

Again, the Israelites did evil in the eyes of the LORD. When King Ehud dies, the Lord sold the Israelites into the hands of Jabin. Sisera was the commander of Jabin's army. Jabin oppressed the Israelites for twenty hard years. During the twenty years, the Israelites were treated cruelly. The Israelites cried to God for help.

Deborah was a prophet, a judge of Israel and the wife of Lapidoth. She rendered her judgments beneath a date palm tree (the Palm of Deborah) between Ramah in Benjamin and Bethel in the land of Ephraim. The Israelites who had disputes/ problems would go to see her at the palm tree so that she could settle to any arguments that occurred between the people who lived in Ramah and Bethel in the hill country of Ephraim.

It is important to remember that the people of Israel had been oppressed by Jabin, the king of Canaan, whose capital was Hazor, for twenty years. Stirred by the wretched condition of Israel Deborah sends a message to Barak and tells him that the Lord God had commanded him to muster ten thousand troops of Naphtali and Zebulun and lead them up to Mount Tabor. Deborah would lead Sisera, who commanded Jabin's army with all his nine hundred chariots and his troops to the Kishon River. There, Barak would kill them. Barak had some trepidations. He informed Deborah that unless she accompanies him, he is not going. Deborah told Barak, "of course I will go with you." She also informed Barak that honor of killing Sisera will not go to Barak, but to a woman. Deborah then went with Barak to Kedesh. There, Barak summoned Zebulun and Naphtali and ten thousand men went up under the command of Barak. Deborah told Barak, "Go! This is the day the LORD has given Sisera into your hands. Has not the LORD gone ahead of you?" So, Barak advanced towards Sisera and his men. God intervened by routing Sisera and all his chariots to Mount Tabor, where Barak and his ten thousand troops were located. As Deborah prophesied, a battle is fought (led by Barak), and Sisera is completely defeated. He himself escapes on foot, while his army is pursued and destroyed.

The story of Deborah is important in Jewish history. Deborah spoke the Word of God. Certainly, Barak deserves credit for the ultimate deaths of Sisera and Jabin, but without Deborah, the Israelites would still be under the rule of a cruel king.

## Lessons learned from Deborah:

1. **God can use whoever He pleases, regardless of gender-** Deborah was a married woman, but God used her to save the Jewish people who were in desperate straits under the rule of Jabin. Deborah convinced Barak to fight and defeat Sisera. God was in control. He used Deborah to defeat Jabin's army. We need to listen to God's word.

2.  **We can forfeit what God has prepared for us-**it is easy for any of us to reject God's plan for us. It is important to say, "yes", when God calls us to do something. He never steers us in the wrong decision or wrong path.

(4)

# Chapter 5

## Delilah-Judges 16

The story of Delilah cannot be told without describing Samson. Delilah was not a "good girl" She was scheming, conniving and insincere. However, she is relevant in Jewish history. Here is a short version of the story of Samson.

Samson was perhaps one of the most flawed and most unusual of the heroes of Israel. His father Manoah, was married to a nameless woman who was childless. An angel of the LORD appeared to her, telling her that she would give birth to a son, whose head is never to be touched by a razor. The angel told the woman that the boy is to be a Nazarite. A Nazarite is a person that to totally dedicated to God. He was to deliver the Israelites from the Philistines. Now Samson has been a problem for the Philistines. He was extraordinarily strong and could not be captured. Every time the Philistines tried to restrain him; Samson would free himself. People were asking him the secret to his strength. He would answer them in riddles. The Philistines were beside themselves. Here is how Delilah becomes a figure in Jewish history.

Samson was a lady's man. He liked women. He eventually fell in love with Delilah. The Philistine rulers went to her and told her to see if she can lure Samson into showing her the secret of his great strength and how the Philistines can overpower him so that they may tie him up and conquer him. The Philistine rulers then told her that each one of them would give her eleven hundred shekels of silver or about 28 pounds.

Well. Delilah could not resist. Did she really love Samson the way her loved her? Evidently not. She said to Samson, "Tell me the secret of your great strength and how you can be tied up and subdued." Samson answered her, "If anyone ties me with seven fresh bowstrings that have not been dried, I'll become as weak and any other man." Delilah told the Philistine rulers what Samson told her. They brought her seven fresh bowstrings that had not been dried and she tied him with them. The Philistine rulers were hiding in the room. She told Samson, "Samson, the Philistines are upon you." Samson easily snapped the bowstrings off. This was not the secret.

Delilah was mad. She told Samson, "You have made a fool of me; you lied to me. Come now, tell me how you can be tied." Samson replied, "If anyone ties me with new ropes that have never been used, I'll become as weak as any other man." Delilah then took new ropes and tied him with them. The Philistine rulers were hiding in the room. Delilah told Samson, "Samson, the Philistines are upon you." Once again, Samson snapped the ropes off his arms as if they were pieces of thread. Delilah said to him that all this time Samson had been making a fool of her and lying to her. So, she asked him again, "Tell me how you can be tied." This time he told her, "If you weave the seven braids of my head into the fabric on the loom and tighten it with the pin, I'll become as weak as any other man." While he was sleeping, Delilah took the seven braids of his head, wove them into fabric and tightened it with a pin. Again, she called to him, "Samson, the Philistines are upon you." Samson awoke and pulled to pin from the loom with the fabric. By now one would think that Samson would realize he is being deceived, but Samson was flawed when it came to women.

Then Delilah used her feminine wiles on Samson. She said, "How can you say, 'I love you' when you won't confide in me? This is the third time you have made a fool of me and have not told me the secret of your great strength. She was nagging him day after day and finally Samson had enough, so he told her everything. He told her that no razor has ever touched his head because he is a Nazarite dedicated to God since he was born. He went on to tell her that if his head were shaved, he would become as weak as any other man. Delilah was satisfied that he was telling her the truth. She sent word to the Philistine rulers, "Come back once more; he has told me everything." The rulers returned with the silver in their hands. After putting Samson to sleep on her lap, she called for someone to shave off the seven braids of his hair. This was the end for Samson. His strength left him. Samson ended up dying, but not after his eyes were gouged out and he was sent to prison. Now Samson's death was quite honorable. He prayed to God to give him back his strength one more time. He died while getting revenge on the Philistines. When he died, he killed many Philistines.

This is the end of the story of Delilah. She is not mentioned anymore. Delilah was a selfish woman. She pretended to love Samson. She wanted the silver. She was a "user." However, in the end, God gave Samson back his strength. He died, but he took many Philistines with him. Delilah did not win!

## Lessons learned from Delilah:

1. **We reap what we sow**-Delilah did not love Samson, she used him, as the Philistines used her. She thought she would bring Samson down,

but Samson died a hero. When he perished, he took many Philistines with him. After Samson's death, Delilah became a "nobody".

2. **Treat people with respect and kindness.** Do not lie. Lies do not end!! They keep going and going. Do not be two-faced or passive aggressive. Be honest with people in a caring, considerate manner.

3. **The love of money is the root of all evil**-this is evident in this story. The thought of all that money brought Delilah down. In retrospect, Samson's death was caused by her.

# Chapter 6

## Dinah-Genesis 34

Dinah was the daughter of Leah and Jacob. One day she was out visiting with some women. She was seen by Shechem. Shechem was the son of Hamor. Hamor was a Hivite and the ruler of that area. When Shechem saw Dinah, he was enamored. He took her and raped her. Shechem loved Dinah. He told his father, Hamor, "Get me this girl as my wife." Hamor, Shechem's father went to talk to Jacob about the situation. When Jacob heard that his daughter had been violated, he did not take any action immediately. His sons had been in the field during the time that Dinah was molested. When they came home, they were told what had happened to their sister. They were furious. But Hamor told the family that his son, Shechem, had his heart set on marrying Dinah. The problem was that this would be an intermarriage from Israelites to non-Israelites. Hamor went on to tell Jacob and his sons to please allow Dinah to marry Shechem. He said, "intermarry with us; give us your daughters and take our daughters for yourselves. You can settle among us; the land is open to you. Live in it, trade in it, and acquire property in it." Then Shechem spoke up and told Dinah's family, "Let me find favor in your eyes, and I will give you whatever you ask. "He went on to plead with her family, telling them that he will pay whatever they want, but allow Dinah to be his wife.

Jacob's sons answered deceitfully. They told Hamor and Shechem that they cannot allow Dinah to marry Shechem because he has not been circumcised (Jewish men were mandated to be circumcised, non-Jewish men did not have that rule to adhere to). They went on to tell Hamor and Shechem that the only way they will agree to this marriage would be that all the males be circumcised. If Hamor agrees to have all the Hivite men circumcised, then Jacob and his sons would agree to the proposal that Dinah can marry Shechem and Jacob's family will settle with the Hivites and live among them. Shechem and Hamor agreed to this response. So Hamor and Shechem immediately went to the gate of their city and spoke to the men. They told the men of the city that they can marry Jacob's tribe's daughters and Jacob's tribe's men can marry their daughters. Everyone will leave in peace. He then went on the tell the men the one caveat, which is that they (the Hivite men) would have to be circumcised. Hamor then added that this was a good deal for the Hivites. Not only would they be able to marry the Israelite daughters, in addition, all the animals would be property of the Hivites because Jacob's family will be living on Hivite property. That clinched the deal for the men. All the Hivite men in the city was circumcised. Three days later, while the men were still in pain from the procedure, two of Jacob's sons, Simeon and Levi, Dinah's brothers killed Hamor and Shechem, took Dinah from Shechem's house and left. Not only that, but Simeon and Levi seized all the flocks and herds and everything else from the city and out of their fields. They carried off all the wealth and all the women and children, taking as plunder everything in the houses. When Jacob found out about this, he was incensed. He was concerned that the Canaanites and the Perizzites, other people living in the area, would join forces against Jacob and his household. Simeon and Levi's response were "should he have treated our sister like a prostitute?"

The story of Dinah is important. Even though she is not a heroine in terms of saving her people, the actions taken on her behalf by her brothers could have caused serious problems for Jacob.

## Lessons learned from Dinah:

1. **Do not give into shame or embarrassment-** The rape situation is egregious and horrendous. I wonder if Dinah willingly wanted to be with Shechem or after the rape, she thought no one else would want her. This issue is not discussed in the Bible. It seems though that Shechem truly did care for Dinah. Times were vastly different than they are now. Rape is NEVER ok. Do not be afraid to confide in someone you could trust if this horrible situation occurred in your life. Do not ever blame yourself for this.

2. **Stand up for what you think is right and best for you-**if Dinah genuinely loved and wanted to be with Shechem, she should have been forthright with her family.

3. **Do not be afraid to confide in someone about issues you are having-**talking to a parent, loved one, friend or even a counselor is beneficial if we are needing guidance.

(5&6)

# Chapter 7

## Esther—The Book of Esther

Esther is a true heroine of the Jewish people. Her story occurred during the time of King Xerxes. Xerxes ruled from his throne is Susa. In the third year of his reign, he gave a huge banquet for all his nobles and officials. This banquet lasted for seven days. This was an extremely elaborate celebration for Xerxes. It was a display of his wealth and power. Queen Vashti was the wife of Xerxes. She was giving a banquet for the women in the royal palace of King Xerxes. On the seventh day of the banquet, while Xerxes was drunk, he commanded the seven eunuchs (a eunuch was a castrated male, usually a servant) to bring before him Queen Vashti so he could show her off to the nobles. Queen Vashti was a beautiful woman thus he wanted to display her beauty. When Vashti's attendants delivered the king's command to her, she refused to come. This refusal infuriated Xerxes. He called his wise men, who were knowledgeable in matters of law and justice. Xerxes wanted to know what can be done with Vashti since she disobeyed the command of King Xerxes. One of the wise men, Memukan, told the King and his nobles, that Vashti's actions were, egregious. Memukan replied, "Queen Vashti has done wrong, not only against the king, but also against all the nobles and the peoples of all the provinces of King Xerxes." He went on to say that if Queen Vashti can defy her husband's commands that other women will follow suit. He continued telling the King that there should not be any disrespect or discord and if action was not taken against Vashti a precedence can be set.

Xerxes was told that a law will be written and cannot be repealed that Vashti is never again to enter the presence of King Xerxes. The purpose of this edict was to show other women never to disrespect their husbands—there will be consequences.

The kings attendants devised a plan. They were going to search for beautiful young virgins for the king. The king was to appoint commissioners in every province of his realm to bring all these beautiful young women into the harem in Susa. They were to be placed under the care of Hegai, the king's eunuch. Hegai was to oversee the women. Beauty treatments were to be administered to the women. Then the young woman who pleases the king the most will be queen. The attendants discussed this plan with Xerxes who liked it and gave his permission to execute the plan.

In the Citadel of Susa, lived a Jew named Mordecai. Mordecai had a cousin named Hadassah, who he raised because she was an orphan. Hadassah was called by another name. It was Esther. Esther had a lovely figure and was beautiful. Mordecai raised Esther after her parents died. When the king's order was proclaimed, many young women were brought to Susa and put under the care of Hegai in the king's harem at the palace. Esther was taken to the king's palace and placed under the care of Hegai. Esther pleased Hegai and won his favor. He was impressed with her. He provided her with beauty treatments and special food. Hegai assigned seven female attendants to Esther. Hegai moved Esther and her attendants to the best area in the harem. Esther did not reveal to anyone that she was a Jew because Mordecai instructed her not to. Every day Mordecai walked back and forth near the courtyard of the harem to check on Esther.

Before a young woman was brought to Xerxes, she had to complete a year of beauty treatments, six months with oil of myrrh and six months perfumes and cosmetics. This is how she would be presented to Xerxes, looking and smelling good. This was the year Esther engaged in. If the woman was not pleasing to Xerxes, she would not return to the king.

Esther did as she was told by Hegai. She did not ask for anything special. Because she did not complain or ask for anything, she was well liked by everyone who saw her. Now it was her turn to be brought to Xerxes. Xerxes was intrigued. He liked Esther more than any other woman brought to him. He placed the crown on her head. Esther was now the queen. Her becoming queen was celebrated with a big banquet. All the king's nobles and officials were at the banquet. They too celebrated that Esther was the new queen.

Mordecai kept vigil at the king's gate. Esther still never told Xerxes or anyone of her background and nationality. She continued to follow Mordecai's instructions. One day while Mordecai was sitting at the gate, he overheard two of the king's officers conspire to assassinate Xerxes. Mordecai told Esther about the plot. Esther in turn told Xerxes. Esther told the king that Mordecai was the person who told her. She gave the credit to Mordecai. When the report was investigated, it was found to be true. The two officers were killed.

Haman was one of the king's nobles. In fact, Xerxes elevated Haman to a higher status than that of the other nobles. Now Haman was very arrogant. Due to his status, everyone at the king's gate bowed down to Haman to pay tribute to him. The king had commanded that everyone kneel when they saw Haman. Mordecai would not bow down to Haman or pay him honor. (In the Jewish religion we need to "know to Whom we kneel" That is God). The royal officials at the king's gate asked Mordecai why he is disobeying the king's edict and not kneeling to Haman. Mordecai would not comply. The officials told Haman that Mordecai refused to kneel or honor him. They were wondering if Haman would excuse this since Mordecai was a Jew. Haman was enraged when he saw that Mordecai would not kneel or pay him honor. When Haman found out that Mordecai was a Jew, he not just wanted to kill Mordecai, but he wanted to kill all the Jews throughout Xerxe's kingdom. In the twelfth year of Xerxes reign, the pur or lot was cast by Haman as to when to carry out his plot to kill all the Jews in the kingdom of Xerxes. When the day was chosen by Haman, he went to talk to King Xerxes. He told Xerxes that "there is a certain people dispersed among the peoples in all the provinces of your kingdom who keep themselves separate. Their customs are different from those of all other people, and they do not obey the king's laws; it is not in the king's best interest to tolerate them. If it pleases the king, let a decree be issued to destroy them, and I will give ten thousand talents (about 375 tons) of silver to the king's administrators for the royal treasury." The king then took his signet ring from his finger and gave it to the that enemy of the Jews, Haman. He told Haman to keep the money and to "do with the people as you please." After this discussion, the royal secretaries were summoned. They wrote out the script of each province with Haman's orders. The edict was written in the name of King Xerxes and sealed with his own ring. Dispatches were sent by couriers to all the king's provinces with the order to "destroy, kill and annihilate all the Jews, young and old, women and children", as well as plundering (stealing) their goods. This decree was to take place on the thirteenth day of the twelfth month of Adar. A copy of the edict was to be issued as law in every province. All the people were informed as what was going to happen to the Jews.

When Mordecai heard about this mandate to have all the Jews killed, he tore off his clothes, put on a sackcloth and ashes and went into the city of Susa wailing loudly. In addition, there was a great mourning amongst the Jews, knowing what was about to happen to them. When Esther's attendants told her about Mordecai, she was most distressed. She sent clothes for him to put on, but he refused. She then ordered one of the king's eunuchs, Hathak, who was assigned to her to talk to Mordecai and find out what was troubling him. Hathak went to Mordecai to talk to him. Mordecai told him everything, including the exact amount of money Haman had promised to pay into the royal treasury for the destruction of the Jews. He also gave Hathak a copy of the text of the edict that detailed the annihilation of the Jews. Mordecai asked Hathak to show the edict to Esther and to tell Esther to plead with the king to stop this destruction and save her people. Hathak went back to Esther and told her what Mordecai said. She told Hathak to tell Mordecai that there was a problem. Anyone who approached the king in the inner court without being summoned will be put to death unless the king extends the gold scepter to them and spares their life. It had been thirty days since Esther was called to go to the king. Hathak went back with this message and communicated it to Mordecai. Mordecai put pressure on Esther. He sent back a message saying that if she remains silent, her family will also perish.

The Jews may be spared in the future, but not this time. Esther's response to Mordecai through Hathak was "to gather all the Jews who are in Susa, and fast for me. Do not eat or drink for three days, night or day. I and my attendants will fast as you do. When this is done, I will go to the king, even though it is against the law. And if I perish, I perish."

On the third day, Esther put on her royal robes and stood in the inner court of the palace, in front of the king's hall. The king was sitting on his royal throne in the hall facing the entrance. He saw Queen Esther standing in the court. He was pleased to see her and held out to her the gold scepter. Esther approached and touched the tip of the scepter. The king then asked Esther what her request was. He told her that even if it were half his kingdom, he would give it to her. She asked Xerxes if he and Haman would come to a banquet that she had prepared for Haman. The king's reply was to bring Haman to the palace at once, so that Esther's request is honored.

The king and Haman arrived at the banquet. As they were drinking wine, the king again asked Esther, "what is your petition? It will be given to you. And what is your request? Even up to half the kingdom, it will be granted." Esther replied, "My petition and my request is this: If the king regards me with favor and if it pleases the king to grant my petition and fulfill my request, let the king and Haman come tomorrow to the banquet I will prepare for them. Then I will answer the king's question."

Haman left happy and full of himself. When he saw Mordecai at the gate, he became enraged because Mordecai did not acknowledge him. Haman did not respond to Mordecai. He went home. He called his friends and his wife, Zeresh to his side. He then boasted about his vast wealth, his many sons and all the ways the king honored him by elevating him to a higher status than that of the other nobles and officials. He then bragged about being the only one invited by Esther to accompany the king to the banquet she was giving the next day. He then added, "But all of this gives me no satisfaction as long as I see that Jew, Mordecai, sitting at the king's gate. His wife and friends spurred him on by saying, "Have a pole set up, reaching to a height of fifty cubits (about 75 feet) and ask the king in the morning to have Mordecai impaled on it. Then go with the king to the banquet and enjoy yourself." Haman loved this suggestion, so he had the pole set up.

That same night Xerxes, unable to sleep was reading a book describing the chronicles of his reign. Now, Xerxes was reading about how Mordecai exposed the two officers who were planning on killing him. He asked "what honor and recognition did Mordecai receive for this act? His attendant replied that nothing had been done to recognize Mordecai for his actions. Just then, Haman arrived to talk to the king about impaling Mordecai. The king summoned Haman into the room. The king asked Haman, "What should be done for the man the king delights to honor?" The arrogant Haman thought the king was talking about him, "who is there that the king would rather honor than me?" This is what Haman was thinking. So, Haman answered the king with this reply, "for the man the king delights to be honor, have him bring a royal robe the king has worn and a horse the king has ridden, one with a royal crest on his head. Then let the robe and the horse be entrusted to one of the king's most noble princes. Let them robe the man the king delights to honor and lead him on the horse through the city streets, proclaiming before him, 'This is what is done for the man the king delights to honor!" The king told this to Haman, "Go at once, Get the robe and the horse and do just as you suggested for Mordecai the Jew, who sits at the king's gate. Do not neglect anything you have recommended." Haman must have been infuriated at this point since he thought he was the one being honored. But it was Mordecai, his mortal enemy! So, Haman did what the king commanded. He robed Mordecai and led him on horseback through the city streets, proclaiming this: "This is what is done for the man the king delights to honor". After this ceremony was over, Haman went home full of grief. He told his wife and friends everything that just happened with Mordecai. His wife and advisors told him that he cannot win over Mordecai so he should leave him alone. But Haman was a prideful man and could not and would not let go of his hatred and jealousy for Mordecai. Meanwhile, the king's eunuchs arrived to take Haman to the banquet that Esther prepared. On the second day of the banquet, the king again asked Esther, "What is your petition? It will be given to you. What is your request? Even up to half the kingdom, it will be granted." Then Esther answered, "If I have found favor with you Your Majesty, and if it pleases you, grant me my life-this is my petition. And spare my people-this is my request. For I have been sold to be destroyed, killed and annihilated. If we merely would have been sold as male and female slaves, I would have kept quiet, because no such distress would justify disturbing the king." King Xerxes asked Esther, "Who is he? Where is he-the man who dared to do such a thing?" Esther replied, "An adversary and enemy! This vile Haman!" At this point, Haman was terrified. The king was furious, He got up and went into the palace garden. Haman already knew what his fate was. He knew the king had probably already made that decision. Haman decided not to follow the king, but to beg Esther for his life. Just as the king returned from the garden to the banquet hall, Haman was falling on the couch where Esther was reclining. The king claimed, "Will he even molest the queen while she is with me in the house?" As soon as that statement was made by Xerxes, Haman's face was covered. Then one of the king's eunuchs told the king, "A pole reaching to a height of fifty cubits stands by Haman's house. He set it up for Mordecai, who spoke up to help the king." The eunuch was acknowledging what Mordecai had done to save the king. The king said, "Impale him on it!" So, they impaled Haman on the very pole he had set up for Mordecai.

The story of Esther is still not over. That same day that Haman was killed, King Xerxes gave Queen Esther the estate of Haman, enemy of the Jews. Esther at this point had told Xerxes how she was related to Mordecai. The king took off his signet ring, which he reclaimed from Haman and presented it to Mordecai. Esther appointed Mordecai over Haman's estate. Esther again pleaded with the king to end the evil plan that Haman devised against the Jews. Then the king extended the gold scepter to Esther. She then asked to king to rescind Haman's order to kill the Jews. She told the king, "For how can I bear to see disaster fall on my people? How can I bear to see the destruction of my family?" The king told Esther to write another decree "in the king's name on behalf of the Jews as it seems best to you and seal it with the king's signet ring-for no document written in the king's name and sealed with his ring can be revoked." In other words, they need to write the decree as they see fit.

Then they are to seal the decree with the signet ring. The king could not revoke Haman's decree because it was already sealed with his ring, but he could order another edict. Again, the royal secretaries were summoned. They wrote out all of the new orders to the Jews. The new edict went to all Jews and officials of the 127 provinces under King Xerxes. Here is what the decree mandated. All Jews in every city were able to assemble and protect themselves. They had the right to destroy, kill and annihilate the armed men of any nationality or province that might attack them and their women and children. In addition, they had the right to plunder the property of their enemies. A copy of this edict was made into law in every province and made known to the people of every nationality so that the Jews could be ready on that day to avenge themselves against their enemy. The day this was to occur was the thirteenth day of the twelfth month of Adar. The same day that Haman planned to destroy the Jews. The couriers riding the royal horses went out and the edict was issued through out Susa.

On the thirteenth day of the twelfth month of Adar, the day the enemies hoped to destroy the Jews, the tables were turned, and the Jews got the upper hand of all the people who hated them. In the city of Susa, the Jews struck down all their enemies, including the ten sons of Haman. The nobles and officials helped the Jews because they were afraid of Mordecai, who had become powerful in Xerxes administration. King Xerxes, in addition, granted Esther's request to carry out the edict in the rest of the king's provinces, as well as impaling Haman's sons.

The remainder of the Jews who were living in King Xerxe's provinces armed themselves for protection against their enemies. The Jews killed seventy-five thousand of their enemies but did not lay hands on their belongings. This occurred on the thirteenth day of the month of Adar and on the fourteenth day they rested and made it a day of feasting and joy. This is the reason for the celebration of Purim. Purim is a time when we observe the day that the Jews got relief from their enemies and turned what could have been a tragedy into a joyful time. Mordecai instructed the Jews to celebrate near and far. So, the Jews celebrated the fact that Haman, mortal enemy of the Jews, who was insistent on killing all the Jews, was himself and his sons impaled. Purim is a festive, but important holiday. We should never forget to celebrate the fact that the Jews who were supposed to die, lived!!

Although, Mordecai is a central figure in this story, if it were not for Esther, the Jews may have had a disastrous outcome. Esther literally risked her life by going to see Xerxes without being summoned. She had the guts to hold a banquet where Haman's plan was revealed. She saved the Jewish people. She was a her-o!

## Lessons learned from Esther:

1. **God can use anyone-**God can use ordinary people to do extraordinary things. Israel was in captivity during this time due to their disobedience to God. Esther was the adopted daughter of a cousin. Esther was just an ordinary Jewish person. In fact, being a Jew set her apart as Jews during that time were frowned upon and scorned. Other than her beauty, she was not special by any means. God used Esther to carry out His plan. God can use any one of us for His plans. We need to submit to His will and be ready to serve Him.

2. **Beauty should not make us boastful**-from all Biblical accounts, Esther was a beautiful woman and with all the beauty treatments she received in one year, it is safe to say that her beauty was probably enhanced. The king was captivated by her beauty, but her eunuch, Hegai, was more impressed with her humble spirit. She never asked for more than was given to her. When she was summoned to the king, she went as is, no more. King Xerxes was impressed with her outward and inward beauty. She never flaunted more than she was. Esther let her faith in God shine through, along with her inner beauty. Some women may have been born with extremely good looks, but if they are prideful, self-centered, arrogant, and uncaring, it does not matter how beautiful someone is. People will see their attitude, not their beauty. God will not shine through them. Remember that God has blessed people with their looks, but it is up to us to treat people with respect, be humble and gracious and remember Who created us!

3. **With God's help, we can step out in faith and fight our fears**-Esther was a Jewish woman. Again, at that time, Jews were vilified. No one, not even the queen could approach the king without being summoned. And do not forget about Haman, who was a member of King Xerxe's cabinet. It was Haman's goal to have all the Jews annihilated. Can you imagine how nervous Esther must have been to approach the king regarding having a banquet to expose Haman? But she did what she needed to do. She prayed to God for guidance and the king welcomed her and agreed

to having the banquet. Haman died on the very spot where he was going to kill Mordecai!! The Jews were saved. When we are faced with an uncertain situation, we need to pray to God, then confidently face those fears.

4. **Our past does not dictate our future-**Esther did not have much. She was an orphan living in a strange land. The thought that she would be a queen probably did not even dawn on her. But wow-did God have a plan for her!! No matter where we come from, where we live or the mistakes we have made, we can put that all in the past and move confidently forward knowing that God has plans for us, for our hopes and our future. Only God can dictate our future. He can take our baggage and make it into a gift—we need to trust in Him.

5. **God places mentors in our life to teach us wisdom-**Mordecai guided Esther throughout the whole process. He gave her sound advice. Mordecai was very loyal to his people. When he heard about Haman's evil plot, he went right to Esther and asked her to go talk to the king. It was sound advice, even though a bit precarious for Esther. Mordecai's advice, from her trusted advisor, saved a nation. We all need God-loving mentors in our life to advise, correct and listen. God places these special people in our lives to help us to follow in His way. If we are facing a struggle, we need to seek the advice of a mentor who will help us to discern what to do and guide us with the Bible. In addition, we too need to mentor others. We can touch the lives of others by acting as a loving guide.

6. **Our strength does not come from us-**Esther's strength did not come from her, but from God. She prayed and fasted. God gave her the strength to save the Jews. When you feel weak. When life's struggles seem overwhelming and you feel like you just cannot do it. Give it to God and let Him do it for you. Let Him fight your battles. Let go and let God. He will fight our battles for us. He, alone, is our strength and stronghold.

7. **God's timing is perfect. Patience is a virtue.** Sometimes we want what we want, and we want it immediately. We need to wait on God's timing. Stop, pray, and wait for God to intervene—He will. When Esther learned of Haman's plan to massacre the Jews, she did not instantly jump up and run to the king. Rather, she prayed, fasted, and waiting for God to prompt her on when to approach the king and how to do it. If Esther had rushed into see the king, Xerxes would not have had the time to read his chronicles and remember that Mordecai exposed the two officers who were planning on killing him. He may not have believed Esther. This, in turn, opened the door for Mordecai to be honored and Esther to ask the king to save the Jewish people.

8. **We can make an impact for generations-**Esther's action saved the Jewish race. We too can make an impact on others. A kind word, holding the door open for someone, not being rude and inconsiderate, even if someone is rude to us, giving up a close parking spot to someone else; there are many things we can do daily to impact others, even things that seem insignificant.

It is up to us to spread the Word of God, even by seemingly insignificant actions.

9. **God is behind the scenes-**God is not specifically mentioned in the Book of Esther, but it is clear He is behind the scenes. God has our backs all the time.

(7)

# Chapter 8

## Eve—Genesis 2 & 3

When God created Adam, He placed him in the Garden of Eden to work it and take care of it. The Garden of Eden was a paradise. Everything anyone could want was there for the taking. The only mandate God told Adam was, "You are free to eat from any tree in the garden, but you must not eat from the tree of the knowledge of good and evil, for when you eat from it you will certainly die." God had formed the all the wild animals and all the birds in the sky. God brought all the animals and birds to Adam. Adam named them. But Adam needed a companion. So, God caused him to fall into a deep sleep and while he was sleeping, He took one of Adam's ribs and then closed the place with flesh. Then God made a woman from the rib He had taken from Adam. God then took the woman to Adam. Adam said, "This is now bone of my bones and flesh of my flesh; she shall be called 'woman', for she was taken out of a man." Adam and the woman were both naked, and they felt no shame.

The woman was walking around in the garden and came upon the serpent. The serpent was craftier than any of the wild animals God created. The serpent said to the woman, "Did God really say, 'You must not eat from any tree in the garden?" The woman said to the serpent, "We may eat fruit from the trees in the garden, but God did say, 'You must not eat fruit from the tree that is in the middle of the garden, and you must not touch it, or you will die.'" The serpent told the woman, "You will certainly not die. For God knows that when you eat from it your eyes will be opened, and you will be like God, knowing good and evil." When the woman saw that the fruit of the tree was good for food and pleasing to the eye, and desirable for gaining wisdom, she took some of it and ate it. She then gave some to Adam who was with her. He too ate some of the fruit from the tree. Then the eyes of both were opened and they realized they were naked. So, they sewed fig leaves together and made coverings for themselves. Then Adam and the woman heard God as He was walking in the garden. Adam and the woman hid from God. God called out to Adam, "Where are you?' Adam answered, "I heard you in the garden and I was afraid because I was naked; so, I hid." God replied, "Who told you that you were naked? Have you eaten from the tree that I commanded you not to eat from?" Adam said to God, "The woman you put here with me-she gave me some fruit from the tree, and I ate it." Then God said to the woman, "What is this you have done?" The woman said, "The serpent deceived me, and I ate it." God was very angry at them both. He cursed woman and told her that her pains during childbirth will be severe and that her husband will rule over her. God also cursed Adam telling him that he will eat the food from the ground, but he will have to work hard to get it. In other words, paradise was over for these two. They would have to sweat and toil for their food. The Lord God banished Adam and Eve from the Garden of Eden. Adam named his wife Eve because she would become the mother of all the living. Eve was the first wife as well as the first mother.

Was Eve to blame for this debacle or was she an innocent victim? You decide.

# Lessons learned from Eve:

1. **Listen to GOD-**when GOD tells us something, we need to listen. Eve was clearly told by God not to eat the fruit from the tree that was in the middle of the Garden of Eden. She defied God, which led to dire consequences. Be attuned to God's Word.
2. **Do not give into temptation-**most of the times, this does not go well. Temptation can make us do things which can be harmful to us and/or harmful to others.
3. **Think before you act. Remember the consequences-**every decision we make influences us and/or someone else. The result can be beneficial or harmful. Think about the consequences of your decisions.
4. **Do not play the "blame game"-**Eve did not take responsibility for her actions. She blamed the serpent. She willingly ate the fruit, knowing she was told not to. It is important to confess our mistakes to God. We need to take responsibility for our actions being right or wrong.
5. **Remember God is in control-**we need to turn our lives over to Him. Eve thought she knew better than God when she made the decision to eat the fruit. Was she trying to usurp God?
6. **Be appreciative of our surroundings-**Eve had it all, then she blew it. Be thankful for the good things in our lives, appreciate the land God gave us, the oceans, lakes, trees, etc. There is beauty all around us. Sometimes we take those things for granted.

(8 & 9)

# Chapter 9
## Hagar-Genesis 2:16 & 21

The story of Hagar is enmeshed with Sarai (Sarah) and Abram (Abraham). Sarai, who was Abram's wife had not borne him any children. In those times, barren women can use another woman as a surrogate. The surrogate's child would become the other woman's child. Since Sarai was barren and wanted to give Abram a child, she told him to sleep with her Egyptian slave, Hagar, so that Sarai can build a family through her. Abram agreed to what Sarai said. Sarai, Abram's wife then took her slave, Hagar and gave her to her husband to be his wife. He slept with Hagar and she conceived. When Hagar knew she was pregnant she became to despise (scorn or ridicule) Sarai. Sarai, in response, blamed Abram. She told Abram, "You are responsible for the wrong I am suffering. I put my slave in your arms, and now that she knows she is pregnant, she despises me. May the LORD judge between you and me." Abram washed his hands of this situation. He told Sarai, "Your slave is in your hands. Do whatever you think best." Sarai mistreated Hagar, so Hagar fled from Sarai. The angel of the LORD found Hagar near a spring in the desert. He asked Hagar, "Hagar, slave of Sarai, where have you come from and where are you going?" Hagar answered, "I am running away from my mistress, Sarai." Then the angel of the LORD told her, "Go back to your mistress and submit to her. I will increase your descendants so much they will be too numerous to count. The angel of the LORD also said to her: "You are pregnant, and you will give birth to a son. You shall name him Ishmael, for the LORD has heard your misery.

He will be a wild donkey of a man; his hand will be against everyone, and everyone's hand against him, and he will live in hostility toward all his brothers. So, Hagar bore Abram a son, and Abram gave the name Ishmael to the son she had borne. Abram was eighty-six when Ishmael was born. When Abram was ninety-nine years old, the LORD appeared to him and told Abram that the God will make a covenant with him and that Abram will be the father of many nations. God changed Abram's name to Abraham. God also told Abraham that Sarai will now be called Sarah and she will have a son by Abraham. God said to Abraham, "I will bless her and will surely give you a son by her. I will bless her so that she will be the mother of nations; kings of peoples will come from her." Abraham was one hundred years old and Sarah was ninety. Abraham laughed to himself and probably was somewhat skeptical. How can someone this old bear children. Abraham then asked God to also bless Ishmael. Then God said to Abraham, "Yes, but your wife Sarah will bear you a son, and you will call him Isaac. I will establish my covenant with him as an everlasting covenant for his descendants after him. And as for Ishmael, I have heard you; I will surely bless him; I will make him fruitful and will greatly increase his numbers. He will be the father of twelve rulers, and I will make him into a great nation. But my covenant I will establish with Isaac, whom Sarah will bear to you by this time next year."

One day the LORD appeared to Abraham while he was sitting at the entrance to his tent. Abraham looked up and saw three men standing nearby. Abraham knew they were angels of the LORD. Abraham offered them rest and food. They agreed. So, Abraham went to Sarah and told her to make some bread, while he found a tender calf to prepare for the three men. While the three men were eating, they asked Abraham, "Where is your wife Sarah?" Abraham replied that she is in the tent. One of the three men said to Abraham, "I will surely return to you about this time next year, and Sarah, your wife will have a son." Sarah happened to be listening at the entrance of the tent. Sarah was laughing to herself. After all, she was ninety and Abraham was one hundred. Sarah thought, "After I am worn out and my lord (Abraham) is old, will I now have this pleasure?" Then the LORD said to Abraham, "Why did Sarah laugh and say, 'Will I really have a child, now that I am old?' Is anything too hard for the LORD? I will return to you at the appointed time next year, and Sarah will have a son." Sarah was afraid and lied to Abraham about laughing, but he said to her, "Yes, you did laugh."

Now the LORD was gracious to Sarah and gave her a son named Isaac. Now we go back to Hagar. Sarah saw that Ishmael was mocking Isaac. Mocking has several meanings. It could mean that Ishmael was rude or that Ishmael was making fun of Isaac in a cruel manner. Whatever happened, Sarah had enough. She told Abraham to "Get rid of that slave woman and her son, for that woman's son will never share in the inheritance with my son, Isaac." Abraham had concerns about sending Hagar and Ishmael away. After all, Ishmael was his son. But God said to Abraham, "Do not be so distressed about the boy and your slave woman. Listen to whatever Sarah tells you, because it is through Isaac that your offspring will be reckoned (numbered). I will make the son of the slave into a nation also because he is your offspring." Early the next morning Abraham took some food and a skin of water and gave them to Hagar. He set them on her shoulders and sent her and Ishmael off. They wandered into the Desert of Beersheba. When the water was gone, Hagar placed Ishmael under one of the bushes. Then she began to cry, "I cannot watch the boy die." God heard Ishmael crying and the angel of the LORD called out to Hagar from heaven. "What is the matter Hagar? Do not be afraid; God has heard the boy crying as he lies there. Lift the boy up and take him by the hand, for I will make him into a great nation." Then God opened Hagar's eyes and she saw a well of water. So, she went and filled the skin with water and gave Ishmael a drink. God was with Ishmael as he grew up. He lived in the desert and became an archer. While he was living in the Desert of Paran, Hagar got him a wife from Egypt.

Sarah lived to be one hundred and twenty- seven years old. Abraham mourned for her when she died and buried her in a cave in the field of Machpelah in the land of Canaan.

Let us discuss Hagar and Sarah. Was Hagar a victim? After all, she was a slave without any opinion. Were Sarah's actions against Hagar due to jealousy and anger that she was unable to bear children? Ancient Hebrew customs allow for surrogacy if the wife was unable to bear children. Also, in those times, it was an embarrassment for a woman not to carry a child. Some of the barren woman were scorned and ostracized. It was a common practice for a barren wife to give her slave to her husband to bear children. The children would be raised by the wife and husband as their own kin. Hagar did not have any input into this situation. Probably her one mistake was being rude and deriding to Sarah. Sarah probably felt angry and jealous that she could not bear children, plus the fact that her husband slept with someone else. All the emotions of jealousy and anger already affected Sarah. Add to the mix was a conniving slave. Sarah probably had enough and could not take it anymore, so she sent Hagar away. But God watched out for Hagar. She went back to Sarah. There is not a discussion in the Bible of the years with Ishmael and Hagar prior to the birth of Isaac. But after Isaac was born, Sarah's full attention went to him. When she saw Ishmael treating her son cruelly, that was it. She had Abraham send him and Hagar away. She did not want Ishmael sharing in the inheritance, but do you think there was more to this reason that Sarah wanted Ishmael gone?

## Lessons learned from Hagar:

1. **Always treat people with dignity and respect-** once Hagar became pregnant through Abraham, she began to belittle and demean Sarai (Sarah). She was haughty and really became a bully. She not only hurt Sarah's feelings, but imbued in Sarah feelings that were akin to hate. Sarah then blamed Abraham for the whole issue when it was her idea to give Hagar to Abraham in the first place. Demeaning others by harsh words or bullying is incongruent with the Word. We are to treat everyone with kindness, even those who are unkind to us. Words can be kind or hurtful. It is important to think before we speak.

   In addition, Sarah was not right either. She compounded the problem by treating Hagar horribly. Sarah did not take the high road in this case. Both she and Hagar contributed to this uncaring, toxic relationship.

2. **The Lord is merciful. Trust in God-**Sarah treated Hagar so dreadfully that she ran away. But God came through for Hagar. Despite how she treated, God took care of Hagar. She produced Ishmael. who God promised to "make him a great nation." When Ishmael was dying of thirst in the wilderness, God heard Hagar crying. Hagar placed Ishmael a distance from her so she would not have to witness his dying. God also was with Ishmael. He sent an angel to Hagar who told her that He will "make Ishmael into a great nation." Suddenly Hagar saw water and saved herself and her son. Even though Hagar did not treat Sarah well, God knew there were two parts to that story. God will come through for us. We need to trust. Even if we make mistakes, He is with us.

3. **Face fears courageously-** instead of running away from difficult situations, ask God for help and guidance. When we face and deal with difficult issues, we receive blessings because we put our trust and faith in God that He will guide and help us through difficult times.

4. **Have an intimate relationship with God-**take your problems to God, talk to Him, pray to Him. God will intervene. It may not be at that exact moment you pray, but He will intercede in your behalf.

5. **God fulfills His promises-**God saved Hagar and Ishmael. He is with us too!!

(10)

# Chapter 10

## Hannah- 1 Samuel 1

Hannah's story is both tragic and a blessing. Hannah was a member of the "barren-women" group. She was in the company of Rachel, Sarah, and Samson's mother.

Hannah's story begins with her marriage to Elkanah. From all accounts it was a happy marriage. Hannah was his first wife, Peninnah his second wife. Peninnah had children, Hannah did not have any children. Every year Elkanah went from his hometown up to Shiloh to worship and offer a sacrifice to God. Eli and his two sons, Hophni and Phinehas, served as the priests of God there. When Elkanah sacrificed, he passed helpings from the sacrificial meal around to his wife Peninnah and all her children, but he always gave an especially generous helping to Hannah because he loved her so much, and because God had not given her children. Peninnah continuously harassed and demeaned Hannah because she was childless and reminding her that she (Peninnah) had children. Hannah was miserable, crying all the time and did not have an appetite. Elkanah was upset, he said to her, "Oh, Hannah, why are you crying? Why aren't you eating? And why are you so upset? Am I not of more worth to you than ten sons?" So, Hannah ate. Then she pulled herself together, slipped away quietly, and entered the sanctuary. The priest Eli was on duty at the entrance to God's Temple in the customary seat. Crushed in soul, Hannah prayed to God and cried and cried—inconsolably. Then she made a vow:

"Oh, God-of-the-Angel-Armies,

If you'll take a good, hard look at my pain,

If you'll quit neglecting me and go into action for me

By giving me a son,

I'll give him completely, unreservedly to you.

I'll set him apart for a life of holy discipline."

While she was praying before God, Eli was watching her closely. Hannah was praying in her heart, silently. Her lips moved, but no sound was heard. Eli jumped to the conclusion that she was drunk. He approached her and said, "You're drunk! How long do you plan to keep this up? Sober up, woman!"

Hannah said, "Oh no, sir—please! I am a woman who is deeply troubled. I haven't been drinking. Not a drop of wine or beer. The only thing I've been pouring out is my heart, pouring it out to God. Don't for a minute think I'm a bad woman. It's because I'm so desperately unhappy and in such pain that I've stayed here so long." Eli answered her ""Go in peace. And may the God of Israel give you what you have asked of him." Hannah responded, ""Think well of me—and pray for me!" she said and went her way. Then she ate and was happy and relieved.

The next morning, they worshiped God and returned home to Ramah. Elkanah slept with Hannah his wife, and God began making the necessary arrangements in response to what she had asked. Before the year was out, Hannah had conceived and given birth to a son. She named him Samuel, explaining, "I asked God for him."

When Elkanah next took his family on their annual trip to Shiloh to worship God, offering sacrifices and keeping his vow, Hannah did not go. She told her husband, "After the child is weaned, I'll bring him myself and present him before God—and that's where he'll stay, for good."

Elkanah said to his wife, "Do what you think is best. Stay home until you have weaned him. Yes! Let God complete what he has begun!"

So, she did. She stayed home and nursed her son until she had weaned him. Then she took him up to Shiloh, also bringing the makings of a generous sacrificial meal—a prize bull, flour, and wine. They first butchered the bull, then brought the child to Eli. Hannah said, "Excuse me, sir. Would you believe that I'm the very woman who was standing before you at this very spot, praying to God? I prayed for this child, and God gave me what I asked for. And now I have dedicated him to God. He's dedicated to God for life." Elkanah and Hannah went home to Ramah. The boy stayed and served God in the company of Eli the priest.

## Lessons learned from Hannah:

1.  **God will always come through-**Hannah prayed for a child-God came through and gave her a son.
2.  **God's timing is perfect-**God is always in control. Samuel was born, Hannah had her son.
3.  **God gives us peace-**when we give our concerns to God, He will take care of them and give us peace.
4.  **It is important to keep your vows-**If you make a promise to God, keep it. God knows what we promised Him. God knows if we renege on our promises to Him.
5.  **God gives grace and joy-**When we leave our burdens to God, He will give us peace. When we are at peace, we can be more joyful, knowing God is in complete control.

(11)

# Chapter 11

## Jael-Judges 4

After Sisera flees Barak's army on foot, he came to the tent of Jael, who was the wife of Heber. Heber and Jabin had an alliance. Because of this, Sisera thought he was safe going to Heber's tent. Jael saw Sisera arriving at the tent to told him not to be afraid and invited him into the tent. When he entered the tent, Jael covered him with a blanket. Sisera told Jael that he was thirsty. He asked for some water. Jael opened a skin of milk, gave him a drink, then covered him back up. Sisera, was frightened. He instructed Jael to stand at the door. He told her that if anyone comes by and asks, "Is anyone in there?", Jael is to say, "no". Jael picked up a tent peg and a hammer and quietly went to Sisera while he was asleep. She drove the tent peg through his temple, and he died. Meanwhile, Barak came by looking for Sisera. Jael went out to meet him. She took Barak into her tent and showed her a dead Sisera. On this same day God intervened with Jabin. He delivered Jabin to the Israelites. Jabin was ultimately destroyed by the Israelites.

Jael is most definitely a heroine. She literally risked her life for the Jewish people. Had she not killed Sisera, he could have regrouped and possibly overthrew Barak and his ten thousand men

## Lessons learned from Jael:

1. **Act on the opportunities God gives us-**God uses anyone! Jael saw an opportunity to save the Jewish people. She had a golden opportunity, but despite the risks, ended the life of an evil man.

2. **God will always accomplish His Word-**It may not be what we perceive it will be, but His will be done at His timing. Because of Deborah and Jael, the Israelites were at peace for several years.

3. **God can choose anyone to fulfill His Word-**God chose women, who in those times, were subservient to men and considered second-class citizens, to accomplish His goals. These second-class citizens allowed the Israelites to be free and at peace.

4. **Choose faith over fear-**Jael was not an Israelite but was a Kenite. This battle had nothing to do with her. She took many risks; what would happen to her if Sisera or Jabin might do to her if they suspected she was going to betray them and what if her husband did not support her? Jael could have feared but had faith. She knew the Israelites were in trouble. She decided to be used to help them. She chose faith over fear. We need to trust in God. He has control of our lives. We cannot allow fear to overtake our trust and belief in God.

(12)

# Chapter 12

## Jezebel-1 Kings 16:29, 31-32, 1 Kings 18:13-42, 1 Kings 19:1-3, 1 Kings 21:1-16, 2 Kings 9

The story of Jezebel is connected to Elijah, but I am focusing on her in this chapter. Jezebel is one of the "bad girls." Jezebel was married to King Ahab. Now Now, King Ahab did more evil than did his predecessor. He was married to Jezebel, who persuaded him to serve and worship Baal. Jezebel always had to be in control and was not pleased with people who challenged her. After marrying Ahab, Jezebel turned him totally against God and towards the belief in Baal and Asherah. She had many prophets of Yahweh killed because they challenged her and the belief of Baal and Asherah. She interfered with the worship of the Hebrew God, she not only encouraged, but almost mandated believing in Baal and Asherah. She disregarded the prophets, Elijah, and Elisha. And again, she killed many prophets of God. She was a destructive force that affected Israel for years.

These evil and tyrannical works prompted the righteous Elijah to seek revenge for the killing of God's prophets. He predicted the encounter of a severe drought as divine retribution against Jezebel. Elijah later had the Baal priests killed after they had failed in a contest with him to see which God would answer their prayers to inflame a bull offering, Baal, or Yahweh. When Jezebel learned of the killing, she furiously vowed to have Elijah killed, forcing him to flee for his life.

Jezebel was a greedy, arrogant person. In addition to killing God's prophets, she was responsible for death of an innocent Godly man named Naboth. Naboth was a civilian who owned a vineyard. Ahab wanted Naboth's vineyard, but Naboth would not relinquish it. Ahab said to Naboth, "Let me have your vineyard to use for a vegetable garden, since it is close to my palace. In exchange I will give you a better vineyard or, if you prefer, I will pay you whatever it is worth." But Naboth replied, "The LORD forbid that I should give you the inheritance of my ancestors." So, Ahab went home, sullen, and angry because Naboth the Jezreelite had said, "I will not give you the inheritance of my ancestors." He lay on his bed sulking and refused to eat. His wife Jezebel came in and asked him, "Why are you so sullen? Why won't you eat?" He answered her, "Because I said to Naboth the Jezreelite, 'Sell me your vineyard; or if you prefer, I will give you another vineyard in its place.' But he said, 'I will not give you my vineyard.'" Jezebel his wife said, "Is this how you act as king over Israel? Get up and eat! Cheer up. I'll get you the vineyard of Naboth the Jezreelite." So, she wrote letters in Ahab's name, placed his seal on them, and sent them to the elders and nobles who lived in Naboth's city with him. In those letters she wrote: "Proclaim a day of fasting and seat Naboth in a prominent place among the people. But seat two scoundrels opposite him and have them bring charges that he has cursed both God and the king. Then take him out and stone him to death.

Jezebel devised a plan to have Naboth accused of blaspheming God. So, the elders and nobles who lived in Naboth's city did as Jezebel directed in the letters, she had written to them. They proclaimed a fast and seated

Naboth in a prominent place among the people. Then two scoundrels came and sat opposite him and brought charges against Naboth before the people, saying, "Naboth has cursed both God and the king." So, they took him outside the city and stoned him to death. Then they sent word to Jezebel: "Naboth has been stoned to death."

As soon as Jezebel heard that Naboth had been stoned to death, she said to Ahab, "Get up and take possession of the vineyard of Naboth the Jezreelite that he refused to sell you. He is no longer alive, but dead." When Ahab heard that Naboth was dead, he got up and went down to take possession of Naboth's vineyard. It does not seem that Ahab had the strength of character to have devised this plan, but his greedy, strong-willed, control-freak wife did. Ahab died fighting the Syrians, but Jezebel continued worshipping and converting people to pray to Baal. She also never changed her demeanor. She still wielded great power over the people.

Meanwhile, Elisha, Elijah's heir, continued to end Baal worship. He anointed Jehu to be king of Israel, an order that prompted civil war because Jehoram, Jezebel's son, then ruled. Jehu was up for the job. He killed Jehoram and sought to overthrow Jezebel and take his place as ruler of Israel. Jezebel knew Jehu was coming. She dressed herself in fancy clothing for the occasion. Looking down from her window, she ridiculed him. Jehu commanded her eunuchs to toss her out of the window. After her fall and death, he ordered that she be buried as a king's daughter, however, it was found that dogs had eaten most of her body, just as Elijah had predicted. Jezebel has come to be recognized as a model of the wicked woman, embodying the characteristics of cruelty, power-hungry, greed, and vanity.

## Lessons learned from Jezebel:

1. **Do not use our strengths and good qualities for evil-**Jezebel was smart, but instead of using her intelligence for pious purposes, she schemed for evil ideals.

   Jezebel had courage and boldness but used those attributes to intimidate others and murder. Jezebel had leadership qualities but used them to control her husband and others. She was assertive but did not use that quality to bring people to God, but the opposite. She turned her assertiveness into aggressiveness and used that quality to turn people against God.

2. **Don't' use power for the wrong reasons-**Jezebel was power hungry and a control freak. She was a murderess. Naboth had a vineyard next to the palace. Jezebel wanted it, but Naboth refused to sell it because it was an inheritance from his father. Jezebel was so determined to get the vineyard for her husband, Ahab, because he wanted it, that she set a series of evil acts in motion that caused Naboth to be killed and she and Ahab to get the vineyard after his death. Jezebel wrote letters to the elders that were filled with false accusations and character assassination.

   Jezebel committed forgery and identity theft by putting King Ahab's seal on the letters she wrote accusing Naboth. She had them people testify that Naboth had cursed both God and the kings. She commanded the nobles and elders of Samaria to "take him (Naboth) out and stone him to death." (1 Kings 10)

Naboth was stoned to death and her husband took his vineyard. She lied, stole, and cheated.

3.  **Serve the right God, not the wrong god-**Jezebel encouraged her husband King Ahab to abandon the worship of God and promote the worship of the Baal and Asherah. Ahab took his wife's advice and the worship of Baal and Asherah rose to a national level as the worship of Yahweh declined.

4.  **We reap what we sow-**Jezebel died a horrible death. Jehu ordered members of Jezebel's eunuchs to throw her out of the window. Her blood splattered on the ground, on the wall, and on the ground. Jehu ordered that her body be buried because she was the wife of a king of Israel. When Jehu's servants went to honor his request, they discovered only her skull, her feet, and the palms of her hands were left behind. The rest of her flesh had been eaten by stray dogs, just as the prophet Elijah had prophesied earlier.

5.  **Always turn to God-**we need to turn to God, not away from Him. We should always encourage people to seek God. Treat people with love and respect. Do not manipulate them and falsely accuse them just to get what you want.

(13)

# Chapter 13
## Jochebed-Exodus 2:1-10

Jochebed was a daughter of Levi and mother of Aaron, Miriam, and Moses. There really is not written much about her specifically in the Bible, but her act and faith in God will always stand out. Her name is first mentioned in Exodus 6:20. She lived in Egypt where the Israelites were enslaved and oppressed. The Pharaoh (probably Ramses II) was becoming concerned because the Israelites had multiplied greatly. In fact, there were so many of them that the land was filled with them. Ramses II was concerned that the Israelites would outnumber the Egyptians, so he gave a decree to the midwives, "When you are helping the Hebrew women during childbirth on the delivery stool, if you see that the baby is a boy, kill him, but if it a girl, let her live." The midwives (which will be discussed later in the book), did not adhere to Ramses decree because they feared God. Ramses than gave this order to all his people, "Every Hebrew boy that is born you must throw into the Nile but let every girl live."

Jochebed gave birth to a son in the middle of Ramses edict. Because of this she hid the baby for three months. When she could no longer hide him, she placed him in a papyrus basket, coated it with tar and pitch. Tar and pitch were used for a coating, so these products may have made the basket watertight. Jochebed than put the child in the basket and put it among the reeds of the Nile. His sister, Miriam, stood at a distance, watching the scenario unfold. Pharaoh's daughter just happened to be going to the Nile to bathe. She saw the basket and sent one of slaves to retrieve it. She opened it and saw the baby. He was crying. She felt sorry for the baby. "This is one of the Hebrew babies", she said. Then Miriam went to Pharaoh's daughter and asked, "Shall I go and get one of the Hebrew women to nurse the baby for you?" Pharaoh's daughter answered, Yes, go." Miriam went and got Jochebed. Pharaoh's daughter said to Jochebed, "Take this baby and nurse him for me and I will pay you."

Jochebed was truly a heroine. She risked her life and her baby's if she was caught by the pharaoh's henchmen. Her faith in God and love for her child usurped any edict. If it were not for her saving Moses, where would the Israelites be now, or would there even be a Jewish people?

## Lessons learned from Jochebed:

1. **Understand and balance the risks and rewards-**always weigh the pros and cons of any decision before making it. Remember that any decision we make has consequences; some positive, some negative. Pray to God for guidance and read His Word. You will receive the answer. Jochebed took a risk and it worked for her, Moses, and the Israelites.

2. **Ask yourself, do the potential rewards outweigh the risks-**will you be able to live with the consequences if they are negative. Jochebed did. It turned out well for her, Moses, and the Israelites.

3. **Do not put all your eggs in one basket—**Miriam was watching the whole scenario, so she was able to intervene on Moses' behalf. Always have a Plan B if Plan A does not work out as you intended or wanted it to.

4. **Be willing to collaborate with others-**Jochebed did collaborate with Pharaoh's daughter to ensure her son lived. It is important to have a good, civil relationship with others, even if you do not care for someone. This is a win-win situation for everyone.

5. **Seek and obtain permission-**Jochebed did not take Moses and home to nurse him. She had permission from Pharaoh's daughter. Our decisions must be based on God's will for us. That means we need to pray an ask for guidance before we take any risks.

6. **Believe, trust, and have faith-**God is in control. It is important to talk to Him, believe in Him and trust Him. Jochebed trusted in God, even in the worst circumstances. God rewarded Jochebed by allowing her to nurse her son and be a part of his life.

(14)

# Chapter 14

## Leah-Genesis 29

This is the story of Leah; Rachel will be discussed later in the book. The story of Leah is both sad but is also one of bravery and perseverance. Leah is the older sister of Rachel and the daughter of Laban. Leah is Rebekah's (wife of Isaac) niece. The background of her story begins with Jacob and with the help of his mother, Rebecca, deceiving a dying and blind Isaac into giving him his twin brother Esau's birthright. Fearful of Esau's wrath he flees to Harran. Harran was Rebekah's home. There he meets his extended maternal family, including Laban, his uncle. Laban has two daughters, Leah, the oldest and her younger sister, Rachel. Jacob immediately is smitten with Rachel, who apparently was beautiful. Leah on the other hand is described as having "weary" or "tired" eyes. The only comparison I can attribute to "tired" or "weary" eyes is that perhaps Leah was cross-eyed, or her pupils were not symmetrical. In any case, Jacob finds Rachel more attractive. Jacob goes to Laban and asks for Rachel's hand in marriage. Jacob told Laban that he (Jacob) would work for him for seven years and in return for the seven years of working for Laban, he would be able to marry Rachel. Laban agreed to this arrangement. After the seven years, Jacob went to Laban and told him that the seven years is up, and he wants Rachel as his wife. Laban made a huge feast to celebrate the impending marriage. However, instead of bringing Rachel to the Jacob, he brought Leah. Jacob made love to Leah. When the morning came, Jacob realized he had relations with Leah, not Rachel. Jacob was not pleased. He confronted

Laban who said, "It is not our custom here to give the younger daughter in marriage before the older one. Finish this daughter's bridal week; then we will give you the younger one also, in return for another seven years of work." So, after the wedding week to Leah was over, Laban gave Jacob Rachel to be his wife. Jacob made love to Rachel. His love for Rachel was greater than his love for Leah. Leah's married life must not have been a happy one knowing that her husband loved her sister more. But God intervened. He saw that Leah was not loved and allowed her to conceive while Rachel remained childless. Even though Rachel was infertile, Jacob still loved her more than Leah. Leah went on to give birth to six sons and a daughter. These were: Reuben, Simeon, Levi, Judah, Issachar, and Zebulun. Sometime later she gave birth to Dinah. Rachel went on to have two sons, whom Jacob favored. Rachel's sons were Joseph and Benjamin. It was obvious to Jacob's other children that Joseph and Benjamin were his favorites. It is hard to imagine what Leah was going through emotionally. Leah more than likely had a husband who did not love her as much as his other wife as well as Rachel's children who he favored over Leah's. I can only imagine that she had to be a strong woman to deal with all this stress.

## Lessons learned from Leah:

1. **Thank God for what we have-**Leah gave thanks to God for allowing her to safely have children.

2. **God did not make every woman a physical beauty-**God does not allow physical beauty or the lack thereof to affect his plans. She gave birth to six of the twelve tribes of Israel. God is above everything and everyone. He uses whom

he wants, when he wants, according to his purposes. Leah had "weak" eyes but look what she accomplished. Just because someone is not physically beautiful, does not mean they cannot be used for great things.

(15)

# Chapter 15

## Miriam- Exodus 2:4, Numbers 12 & 20

Miriam was the daughter of Amram and Jochebed; she was the sister of Aaron and Moses, the leader of the Israelites in ancient Egypt. Because the Jews were procreating at an enormous rate, the pharaoh of Egypt became alarmed. He decrees that all male Israelite babies are to be drowned, Moses's mother saves him by placing him on the Nile in a basket. Moses's sister, Miriam stood on the bank of the river to find out what would happen to the infant. And when the pharaoh's daughter discovers the basket, and realizes that it must be a Hebrew child, Miriam is quick to act. She offers to get a Hebrew nursemaid for the baby. She gets her and Moses's mother as the nursemaid.

Later, Miriam is described as a prophetess. Miriam is important because she led the women in singing their own song of praise which was in conjunction with the Song of the Sea that Moses and the Israelites sang after the Egyptian Army was destroyed at the Sea of the Reeds. "Miriam the prophetess, Aaron's sister, took a timbrel in her hand, and all the women came out after her with timbrels and dances. And Miriam called out to them, "Sing to the Lord, for very exalted is He; a horse and its rider He cast into the sea." (Exodus 15: 20-21) She was inspiring and gave God the credit for leading the Israelites' safely out of Egypt. She is designated as one of the seven major female prophets of Israel. She accompanied Moses and Aaron as they led the Jews out of Egypt. Miriam was a key player. Miriam was probably an early feminist. While Moses was teaching the men God's Laws, Miriam was teaching the women.

Miriam, I am guessing was more than likely a strong-willed, self-confident woman. Her confidence did have a downside. She may have been outspoken as was the case when she criticized Moses because he had married a Cushite. A Cushite was a dark-skinned person. However, Miriam's anger towards Moses's Cushite wife may have been a ruse. Miriam and Aaron said, "Has the Lord spoken only through Moses? Hasn't he also spoken through us?" It appears that maybe both Miriam and Aaron were jealous. Because of her role in leading the people out of Israel, she may have felt excluded in God's relationships. Her bitterness and envy got the best of her. God brought her, Moses, and Aaron to the tent of the meeting. At the tent, God came down in a pillar of cloud; he stood at the entrance of the tent and summoned Aaron and Miriam. He chastised both Miriam and Aaron. God reaffirmed His relationship to Moses because of his faithfulness. He went on to tell Miriam and Aaron that he was not pleased that they criticized Moses. When the cloud lifted from the tent, Miriam's skin was leprous-it became white as snow. Aaron asked Moses to talk to God to remove the skin condition from Miriam. God said "If her father had spit in her face, would she not have been a disgrace for seven days? Confine her outside the camp for seven days; after that she can be brought back. Miriam was confined outside the camp for seven days. The Jews could not proceed to the promised land until her seven days of exile were over.

One must ask; Aaron was also involved in criticizing Moses. Why was he not punished as well? One reason can be that Miriam instigated the "mini revolt" and asked Aaron to support her. In the Bible, Miriam is named before Aaron at the start of the account; "Miriam and Aaron began to talk against Moses." Since she initiated the complaint against Moses, she received the greater punishment. In this case, God was just. She started the problem; she holds more accountability.

Another explanation is because Aaron was a high priest. God spared Aaron to ask God to intercede on Miriam's behalf and appreciate Moses with a renewed recognition and understanding of him as God's representative. Aaron said to Moses, ""Please, my lord, I ask you not to hold against us the sin we have so foolishly committed." So, Moses, in turn asked God to "please heal her.' And we know that God said "no". Miriam had to be exiled for seven days. If Aaron were struck with a defiling skin condition, it would have interfered with his ability to perform his role as chief priest. Thus, God spared him.

Miriam died and was buried at Kadesh, an area where there was no water there and the whole Israelite community was complaining.

## Lessons learned from Miriam:

1. **Have courage**-look at what Miriam did to not only save her brother, but the Israelites as well. God tells us- *"Be strong and courageous. Do not be afraid or terrified because of them, for the Lord your God goes with you; he will never leave you nor forsake you." – Deuteronomy 31:6*
2. **Be a good sibling**-stand up for, guide and support your sibling. My mother said when her and my dad are gone, it will just be me and my brother. She was right. Both my parents have passed and thank God, I have a strong and loving relationship with my brother.

3. **Be thankful for our trials as well as good fortune-**we need to be thankful for the little things that we tend to take for granted, food, shelter, family, health, the beauty of flowers, the ocean, trees, etc. We also need to thank God for tribulations in our lives. When bad things happen, is when we realize that God is with us.

4. **Be a leader-**Miriam taught the women about God and the Laws. When the Jews were led out of Egypt, she did not just stop there. She continued working with the women, inspiring them, and guiding them to God. Lead people in the right direction. If you see someone doing something wrong and you feel safe, talk to them.

5. **Use your gifts for God's glory-** we all have strengths. God gave us these gifts. Some people can sing, some can play instruments, some are good stay-at-home parents. Whatever gift God bestowed upon us is for a reason. Miriam discovered that she had been given the gift of prophecy and used this gift to help lead the Israelites to the Promised Land, along with her brothers, Moses, and Aaron.

6. **Do not whine and complain-**God does not want to hear us complain. Miriam was a faithful servant but developed a bitter heart due to jealousy. We need to be grateful for what we have and where we are. If our life takes a turn for the worse, talk to God, talk to a clergy, talk to a friend, physician, or someone who can best help. Ask God where or who you need to turn to besides Him. He will guide you. It is God's will that we be happy and content (if everything is well) with where we are.

7. **Do not gossip or malign others-**The tongue is the worst organ. It can build people up or tear people down. Someone can be hurt by gossip or badmouthing. In some cases, it can lead to an unimaginable conclusion. Something you say to someone, can ultimately and in some cases may cause that person to end their life.

8. **Faith is blessing for now and future generations-** it is important that we teach our children about God and living a Godly life. Faith begins at home. What Miriam did by teaching women about God's Laws, helped secure the future of the Jewish people.

(16)

# Chapter 16

## Naomi and Ruth-The book of Ruth

Because these two women's story are so intertwined, I must write about them together.

The story of Naomi is one of both tragedy and joy. Naomi was married to Elimelek. Naomi and Elimelek had two sons, Mahlon and Kilion. They were originally from Bethlehem in Judah, but due to a famine they moved to Moab. Elimelek died. Naomi was left with her two sons. Both Mahlon and Kilion married Moabite women, Orpah and Ruth. The family lived in Mob for about ten years. Mahlon and Kilion both died, and Naomi was left with her two daughters-in-law.

Naomi heard that the Lord was providing food for His people in Bethlehem (alleviating them from the famine), so she and her daughters-in-law prepared to move back to Judah. Naomi said to Orpah and Ruth, "Go back each of you to your mother's home. May the LORD show you kindness, as you have shown kindness to your dead husbands and to me. May the LORD grant that each of you will find rest in the home of another husband." Then Naomi kissed her daughters-in-law goodbye. Both Orpah and Ruth cried and said, "We will go back with you to your people." But Naomi proceeded to explain to them the futility of going back to Judah with her. She told them, "Am I going to have any more sons, who could become your husbands? I am too old to have another husband. Even as I thought there was hope for me-even if I had a husband tonight and then gave birth to sons, would you wait until they grew up?" Logically, both Orpah and Ruth would be much older than any of Naomi's sons. She then told them that, "this is more bitter for me than for you because the LORD'S hand has turned against me!" She was referring to the loss of her husband and her sons.

Both Orpah and Ruth wept again. Orpah kissed Naomi goodbye and went back to her people and their gods. Ruth on the other hand, would not leave Naomi. Naomi kept pressuring Ruth to go back to her people and their gods. But Ruth would not leave. "Don't urge me to leave you or turn back from you. Where you go, I will go, and where you stay, I will stay. Your people will be my people and your God, my God. Where you die, I will die and there I will be buried. May the LORD deal with me ever so severely, if even death separates you and me." Naomi realized she was not going to persuade Ruth to leave her. Both women continued to Bethlehem. When they arrived in Bethlehem, the whole town was surprised to see them. The women said, "Could that be Naomi?" Naomi told them to call her Mara, not Naomi because "the Almighty has made my life very bitter." They arrived in Bethlehem just in time for the harvesting of barley. It just so happens that Naomi has a relative who lived in Bethlehem, Boaz. Boaz was kin to Elimelek. Boaz was of the family's guardian-redeemers. A guardian-redeemer was a close influential relative to whom members of an extended family could turn to for help.

Since it was barley harvesting season, Ruth told Naomi that she would go to someone's field who would not have any objections to her picking up leftover barley. Naomi gave Ruth approval, so off she went. Ruth entered a field and began gleaning or gathering leftover barley. As it turns out, the field was gleaning in happened to belong to Boaz. Boaz happened to arrive at his field probably to see how the harvesting was going. After he greeted is harvesters, he happened to see Ruth. He asked his harvesters if any of them knew who she was. The overseer told Boaz that Ruth was the Moabite woman who came back from Moab with Naomi. She then asked permission from Boaz to continue gleaning barley in his field. Boaz told her not to glean in any other field, but to stay with him. He told her to stay with the other women who work for him and follow the women. He told her she would be safe from the advances of his workers and essentially told her that when she needed water, to go and get a drink form the water jars. Ruth was humbled and asked Boaz what she has, as a foreigner, done to deserve such treatment. Boaz told her that he had heard of all the things she had done for Naomi, as well as leaving her family and homeland to live with strangers who were not of her culture. He told her may the LORD of Israel repay her for her kindness and loyalty to Naomi. Ruth thanked Boaz and told him that his words put her at ease. She then ate with some roasted grain with the harvesters. Boaz told his men that Ruth can take all the barley she needs. Ruth gleaned the field until evening. She gathered an ephah of barley or about 30 pounds. She carried it and the leftover roasted grain back to Naomi. Naomi asked Ruth where she gleaned the barley. Ruth said that she gleaned it at a field owned by Boaz. Naomi was shocked and thrilled. She told Ruth that Boaz is a close relative. Then she told Ruth to stay where she was and to stay close to the women who worked for Boaz. Ruth and Naomi ended up living together.

After a while, Naomi said to Ruth, "My daughter, I must find a home for you, where you will be well provided for."

She told Ruth that Boaz will be winnowing or examining the barley on the threshing floor that evening. She told Ruth to wash up, dress nicely, put on some perfume and go to the threshing floor. But do not, she told Ruth, let Boaz know she was there until he finished eating and drinking. Naomi continued telling her that when Boaz lays down "go and uncover his feet and lie down. He will tell you what to do." Ruth agreed and did everything Naomi instructed her to do. When Boaz finished eating and drinking, he went to lie down. Naomi came to him uncovered his feet and laid down. In the middle of the night, something startled Boaz. He woke up and found Ruth laying at his feet. He asked her who she was. She told him. Boaz was pleased. He complimented her on not chasing after younger men whether rich or poor. He told her that he will do for her what she asks because she was a woman of noble character. Boaz went on to tell Ruth that even though he is the family's guardian-redeemer there is someone more closely related to the family than he is. He told her that he would talk to this person and will ask if he wants to fulfill his duty Ruth's guardian-redeemer. If this man wanted to be Ruth's guardian-redeemer, good, if he did not, then Boaz would do it. She laid at Boaz's feet throughout the night. The next morning, Boaz asked Ruth to bring him her shawl. He measured out some barley and put it in her shawl for her to carry back to Naomi. Back home, Naomi asked Ruth what happened. Ruth told her everything and then showed her the barley that Boaz had sent back. Naomi told Ruth to sit and wait to see what happens with this other guardian-redeemer.

Now, Boaz went to the town gate to wait for the other guardian-redeemer. Boaz called the man over to talk to him along with ten elders of the town to witness the discussion. He explained to the man about Naomi who was married to their relative Elimelek and who wanted to sell the piece of land that belonged to him. He asked the man if he wanted to buy the land (redeem) or not. The man did want to redeem it. Boaz went on to tell him that "on the day you buy the land from Naomi, you also acquire Ruth the Moabite, the dead man's widow, in order to maintain the name of the dead with the property." In other words, the man had to marry Ruth. The redeemer, at that point, did not want the land, claiming that buy marrying Ruth he could be endangering his own estate. The reason for this is not mentioned in the Book of Ruth. One could suppose that buy marrying a Moabite, could potentially cause some fiscal complications for him. He told Boaz to redeem the land himself. The deal was sealed by the redeemer removing his sandal. During these times, for the redemption and transfer of property to become final, one party must remove his sandal. This was the method of legalizing transactions. The redeemer removed his sandal and told Boaz, "Buy it yourself." Boaz announced to the ten elders, "Today you are witnesses that I have bought from Naomi all the property of Elimelek, Kilion and Mahlon. I have also acquired Ruth the Moabite, Mahlon's widow as my wife, in order to maintain the name of the dead with his property, so that his name will not disappear from among his family or from his hometown. Today you are witnesses!"

Boaz took Ruth and made her his wife. They had a son named Obed. Obed was the father of Jesse and Jesse the father of David and Naomi was a happy grandmother.

# Lessons learned from Naomi and Ruth:

1. **God can take a hopeless situation and turn it into something magnificent**-the story begins with famine and the death of Naomi's husband and sons and Ruth and Orpah's husbands. Ruth would not leave her mother-in-law. God rewarded her loyalty. Not only did she remarry but became the great grandmother of David.

2. **Ruth was a Moabite**-During this time in Israelite history the Moabites were considered inferior. In selecting Ruth, God chose an "inferior" woman to be responsible for the lineage of Israel.

3. **No one is insignificant**-anyone can be used for God's glory

(17)

# Chapter 17
## Rachel-Genesis 29-36

The story of Rachel, like her sister Leah, is one of both tragedy and happiness. I discussed in the chapter about Leah, the meeting of Jacob and Rachel. In order for Jacob to marry Rachel, Laban told Jacob that he had to work for him for another seven years. Jacob agreed to this arrangement. After the bridal week with Leah, Laban gave Jacob Rachel to be his wife. Laban also gave his servant Bilhah to Rachel to be her attendant. Jacob made love to Rachel. He loved Rachel more than he loved Leah. Leah was conceiving child after child, but Rachel remained childless. When Rachel saw how many children Leah was having, she became jealous and told Jacob, "Give me a child or I'll die." Jacob became angry with her and told her, "Am I in the place of God, who has kept you from having children?" She could not handle the fact that her sister was having all those children and she could not. So, she gave Jacob her servant Bilhah. She told Jacob to sleep with Bilhah so that "she can bear children for me and I too can build a family through her." In essence, Bilhah was a surrogate mother. It was acceptable for Bilhah to birth the child and Rachel raise it as her own. Jacob slept with Bilhah. She conceived and gave birth to a son. Rachel felt vindicated. God had listened to her plea. Now she has a son who she named Dan. Jacob again slept with Bilhah, she conceived and bore another son. Rachel's comment was, "I have had a great struggle with my sister, and I have won. She named this son Naphtali.

At this point, Leah was not conceiving any more children. She noticed what was happening with Bilhah, so she gave her servant, Zilpah to Jacob to sleep with. Zilpah bore Jacob two sons. Now Leah was happy. I am adding this so that my summary about Rachel will make sense.

Meanwhile, back to Rachel. She still longed for her own biological children. God remembered Rachel and allowed her to conceive. She became pregnant and gave birth to Joseph. After Rachel had given birth to Joseph, Jacob's other seven years of working for Laban was complete. Joseph went to talk to Laban. He told him that it was time for him to go back to his homeland. Laban was not pleased and argued with Jacob. But God intervened and told Jacob to go back to the land of his family. He told Rachel and Leah what God had told him to do. Since Laban had not given his daughters their inheritance, neither Rachel nor Leah had an issue with leaving their father. Before they left Rachel stole her father's idols and hid them in her camel's seat cushion. Jacob was unaware that Rachel had taken Laban's idols.

So, Jacob loaded up his wives, their servants, and children on camels. Without informing Laban, he took them and his livestock and headed to the land of Canaan. Again, this is a story about Rachel not Jacob, therefore, I will skip the long section regarding Laban and Jacob. Laban decided to pursue Jacob because Jacob left in a hurry, did not let Laban know he was leaving, and did not allow him to say goodbye to his family. He also found out that his idols were missing. He questioned Jacob as to why did he steal his gods? Jacob did not know anything about stolen gods. He told Laban to go search all the tents in search of his idols. Laban went into Jacob's tent, into Leah's tent plus the tents of Bilhah and Zilpah but found nothing. Lastly Laban went into Rachel's tent. Remember that Rachel had hidden the idols inside her camel's saddles and was sitting on them. Laban, of course did not find the idols in Rachel's tent. When he went out of Rachel's tent, he saw his daughter sitting on her camel. She told her father, "Don't be angry my lord, that I cannot stand in your presence; I'm having my period. Laban could not search any farther.

Jacob and Laban ended their bitterness towards each other, and Jacob proceeded home. During the journey to Canaan, near Ephrath, Rachel began to give birth but had great difficulty. Right before her death, the midwife told Rachel that she had given birth to another son. As she breathed her last breath, she named her son Ben-Oni, but Jacob changed his name to Benjamin. Rachel was buried on the way to Ephrath (near Bethlehem) Over her tomb Jacob set up a pillar.

**Why did Rachel take her father's idols?** There are numerous theories:

1. One theory is that Rachel did not want her father to pray to idols.
2. Another theory is that the idols had magical powers and Rachel did not want Laban to know what direction they were taking back to Canaan.
3. Maybe she wanted an extra layer of protection, she believed in God, but perhaps she stole the idols for emotional security. (18 & 19)

## Lessons learned from Rachel:

1. **God's timing-**God allowed Rachel to conceive, but it was His timing. She gave birth to Joseph, who saved his family from famine. He grew up to be a leader.

2. **No one wins with jealousy-**to be jealous is sinful. Her and Leah had a sibling rivalry, but by Rachel nagging and getting angry with Jacob, solved nothing.
3. **Do not be revengeful-**Trust in God. He is in control.
4. **Be grateful and satisfied with what you have-**it is fine to strive for more, but do not allow jealousy and greed to overtake your ambitions.
5. **Love one another-**even if you are experiencing emotions and feelings that are not congruent with God's teachings—be kind and caring.

(20-21)

# Chapter 18

## Rahab-Joshua 2 & 6:22

Rahab's story is one of courage, faith, and sacrifice. Rahab's story begins when Joshua sent two spies to scope out Jericho. Jericho was a sinful city. God told Joshua to destroy the city and all its inhabitants. The two spies came to Rahab's house in Jericho to stay after their travels. Rahab's house was built against the town wall with the roof almost level with the ramparts (a wall-like barrier). The house had a stairway leading up to a flat roof that looked like it was a continuation of the wall. Rahab was a prostitute, so the fact that her house was built against the way it was is significant to her story. It was easy for everyone in Jericho to see who was coming and leaving her house of ill repute.

Rahab had heard through her patrons about what God had done for the Israelites in Egypt by the Exodus and the parting of the Red Sea, as well as the overthrow of Og and Sihon. When the spies came to stay at her house, she was more than willing to let them stay. However, because of the way her house was built, she knew it was only time before the king of Jericho would know they stayed at her house. Rahab knew that these two men were different than the other men who stayed at her house. These were men of God, not men coming for favors. These two men had a mission. That was to overthrow Jericho. Rahab devised a plan so that neither she nor the two spies would get caught. She hid the two spies on her roof under the stalks of flax. And of course, the king of Jericho was told that some of the Israelites have come to Jericho to spy out the land. He sent a message to Rahab,

"Bring out the men that came to your house, because they have come to spy out the whole land." With the men safely hidden, she replied, "Yes, the men came to me, but I did not know where they had come from. At dusk when it was time to close the city gate, they left. I don't know which way they went. Go after them quickly. You may catch up with them." Being that Rahab's house was one of ill-repute, this seemed like a plausible explanation. The men set out looking for the spies. They went on the road that led to the fords of the Jordan. As soon as the men had left the city, the gate was closed.

Rahab then went up to the roof and told the two spies that she was aware that God had sent them to Jericho. The people of Jericho were very fearful of what was about to happen to them. She continued to tell them that, "We have heard how the LORD dried up the water of the Red Sea for you when you came out of Egypt, and what you did to Sihon and Og, the two kings of the Amorites east of the Jordan whom you completely destroyed. When we heard it, our hearts melted in fear and everyone's courage failed because of you, for the LORD your God is God in heaven above and on the earth below." She then asked the two spies "to swear by the LORD that you will show kindness to my family because I have shown kindness to you." She asked the men to give her a sign that they will spare the lives of her father and mother, sisters, and brothers and all that belong to them (her extended family) and that they will all be spared from a certain death. The men told her, "Our lives for your lives. If you don't tell what we are doing, we will treat you kindly and faithfully when the LORD gives us the land." So, Rahab let the two men down by a rope through the window of her house. She told them, "Go to the hills so the pursuers will not find you. Hide yourselves there for three days until they return and then go on your way." Before the spies left, they told her that the oath they swore to her will not be adhered to unless when they enter the land, Rahab had tied a scarlet cord in the same window which they had escaped from. The spies told her to hang, "this scarlet cord." She also had to bring her father, her mother and all her family into her house. If any of them went outside into the street their blood will be on their own heads and the spies will not be responsible for what happened. As for her family that remained in her house, if anything happened to them, the spies would take responsibility. They finally told her that if anyone finds out what they are doing the oath is null and void. Rahab agreed. The spies left and Rahab tied the scarlet cord out the window. The meaning of this section is that in order for Rahab and her family to avoid death due to the destruction of Jericho, there were certain mandates she had to do: tie a scarlet cord out the window and bring her whole family to her house.

The spies left and safely returned to Joshua. Jericho, of course was overthrown by the Israelites. Joshua told the two spies to "Go to the prostitute's house and bring her out and all who belong to her in accordance with your oath to her." So, the two spies went and brought out Rahab, her father, her mother, her brothers, sisters and her extended family. They put them in a place outside the camp of Israel. They were safe. After Rahab and her family were removed from Jericho, the whole city was burned, except Rahab and her family.

Rahab took a huge risk by hiding the spies and making a deal with them. She and her whole family could have been killed, but her belief in God superseded her fear.

The red cord could be a similarity to the lamb's blood on the Israelites houses in Egypt. God passed over those houses with the lamb's blood. (22)

In the end, Rahab married Salmon from the tribe of Judah, and they had a son named Boaz. Boaz married Ruth and subsequently gave birth to Jesse. Jesse is the father of David. Rahab is a most important woman in the Bible. She is in the lineage of David.

## Lessons learned from Rahab:

1. **Always believe in God-**Interestingly enough, Rahab was not an Israelite, but due to what she heard from her guests, believed in God. She had an opportunity to show her trust and belief in God by assisting the spies with their mission. She risked her and her family's lives. She showed great faith by believing in God.
2. **Stand up for God-**we, like Rahab, need to do what is right by God and stand up to people who are trying to sway us away from God.
3. **Do not allow past mistakes to shape our future-**move forward and trust in God to take care of us.
4. **Leave a legacy of faith and obedience-**we need to teach our children to believe in God and follow His ways. We need to do good deeds and treat people with kindness and respect, even if we do not care for someone.

(23)

# Chapter 19

## Rebekah-Genesis 24, 25 and 27

Because of the interconnection of Isaac, Jacob, and Esau, I had to include them in the story, but the summary will discuss Rebekah only. The story of Rebekah is in some ways like that of Rachel in that both women were at an area where there was water (a well and a spring) when they met their prospective spouses, as well that both women were childless. The story of Rebekah also borders on the role of motherhood. Rebekah favored one son, while Isaac favored another. Jacob also favored two sons over the other.

The story of Rebekah begins with the aging of Abraham. Abraham is very old and tells the senior servant of his household to go back to Abraham's homeland and find a wife for Isaac who is part of his family. Abraham made it very clear that Isaac does not marry a Canaanite woman. The servant obliges Abraham and sets off for Abraham's birthplace, Aram, Naharaim. Abraham sent along ten camels filled with jewelry, clothing, and other good things. The servant left. He stopped at the town of Nahor and had the camels kneel by the well. The servant knew that women be drawing water out of that well. The servant prayed to God, "LORD, God of my master Abraham, make me successful today, and show kindness to my master Abraham. See, I am standing beside this spring, and the daughters of the townspeople are coming out to draw water. May it be that when I say to a young woman, 'Please let down your jar, that I may have a drink, and she says, 'Drink, and I'll water your camels too, let her be the one you have chosen for your servant

Isaac. By this I will know that you have shown kindness to my master." Before he finished praying, Rebekah came out with her jar on her shoulder. Rebekah's brother was Laban. Her father was Bethuel who was Abraham's nephew. Rebekah was beautiful and a virgin. Being a virgin was an important aspect to first marriages in those times. Rebekah went down to the spring to fill her jar. As she was coming up from filling her jar, the servant said, "Please give me a little water from your jar. ""Drink my lord, she said." She lowered her jar and gave the servant a drink. After she had given him a drink she said, "I'll draw water for your camels too, until they have had enough to drink." Rebekah ran back to the well to draw more water for the camels. The servant watched her to make sure she was the woman God had wanted for Isaac. When he was convinced, the servant took out a gold nose ring and two gold bracelets. The servant asked Rebekah who she was. She explained that she was the daughter of Bethuel, the son of Nahor. She then invited the servant to spend the night.

While he thanked God for the successfulness of his journey and how God did not forget Abraham, Rebekah ran home and told her family what transpired at the well. Her brother Laban hurried out to meet the man. As soon as he saw the nose ring and the bracelets on his sister's arms, he went to the servant and said, "Come, you are blessed by the LORD, I have a place for you and your camels." The servant followed Laban. The camels were unloaded and set up with straw and fodder (food). Then the servant went in the house. A meal was placed in front of him, but he would not touch it until he told his story. He told Laban, that he was sent by Abraham, who had become wealthy. He went on to tell the story of Sarah, who bore him a child at an old age. He then continued by saying that Abraham did not want his son marrying a Canaanite woman, but instead marry one from his own family. He went on to talk about how he prayed to God for a sign which did occur at the spring. When he finished telling his story, both Laban and Bethuel said, "This is from the LORD; we can say nothing to you one way or the other. Here is Rebekah: take her and go and let her become the wife of your master's son as the LORD has directed." The servant was grateful that there was not any conflict. Laban and Bethuel called Rebekah in the room and asked her if she is willing to go with the servant and be Isaac's wife. Rebekah agreed. Rebekah left her family to make the journey to Isaac and Abraham. Before she left, her family blessed her and said, "Our sister, may you increase to thousands upon thousands, may your offspring possess the cities of their enemies." This prayer certainly did come to fruition!!

Rebekah and her attendants then left for Isaac. One day, Isaac went out to the field to meditate. As he looked up, he saw the camels approaching. Rebekah spotted Isaac and asked who he was. The servant explained to her that Isaac was his master. The servant then explained to Isaac who Rebekah was and about his journey. Isaac took Rebekah into Sarah's tent and married her. Isaac was 40 years old when he married Rebekah. Rebekah was having some problems conceiving. Isaac prayed to the LORD on behalf of his wife. The LORD answered his prayer and Rebekah became pregnant. The babies jostled each other inside her. She probably was frightened, not knowing what is happening to her baby. She went to talk to the LORD who told her, "Two nations are in your womb, and two peoples from within you will be separated; one people will be stronger than the other, and the older will serve the younger." At least Rebekah knew she was having twins. When the time came for her to give birth, twin boys were delivered. The first one to come out was red and hairy, they named him Esau. After this his brother came out, with his hand grasping Esau's heel, so he was named Jacob. It almost seems like Jacob was trying to push Esau out of the way so he could be delivered first, but that is another story. The boys grew up. Esau was a hunter a man of the open country, while Jacob was content to stay home.

Here is where the possible parenting skills come into play. Isaac favored the outdoorsman Esau, while Rebekah favored the quieter Jacob. One must wonder if both boys knew they were favored by different parents. Did Rebekah treat Esau different than Jacob? The same with Isaac, was there blatant favoritism shown on Esau's behalf? How did this affect their childhood and adulthood?

One day Jacob was cooking stew. Esau came in the house famished. He said to Jacob, "first sell me your birthright." Esau said, Look, I am about to die. What good is a birthright to me?" So, Esau swore an oath and gave up his birthright. Jacob then gave Esau the stew. Esau finished eating.

Several years pass. Esau married a Hittite woman. This marriage caused grief for Isaac and Rebecca. Isaac grew old and along with aging became blind. One day he called for his older son Esau. Esau answered his father, "I am here." Isaac told him, "I am an old man and don't know the day of my death. Now then, get your equipment-your quiver and bow-and go out to the open country to hunt some wild game for me. Prepare me the kind of tasty food I like and bring it to me to eat, so that I may give you my blessing before I die." Rebekah overheard the whole conversation. When Esau left for the open country, she said to Jacob, "Look, I overheard your father say to your brother Esau, 'Bring me some game and prepare me tasty food to eat so that I may give you my blessing in the presence of the LORD before I die. Now my son, listen carefully and do what I tell you: Go to the flock and bring me two choice young goats, so I can prepare some tasty food for your father; just the way he likes it. Then take it to your father to eat, so he may give you the blessing before he dies." Jacob voiced his concern to his mother, telling her that, "Esau is a hairy man, while I have smooth skin. What if my father touches me? I would appear to be tricking him and would bring down a curse on myself, rather than a blessing." Rebekah told him, essentially not to worry that she would take the blame for any repercussions. She said, "Let the curse fall on me."

Jacob complied and brought his mother two choice goats. Rebekah prepared the food just the way Isaac liked it. Then Rebekah took some of Esau's best clothes and put them on Jacob. She also covered his hands and the smooth part of his neck with the goatskins. Jacob went to his father and gave him the food. Isaac questioned to validity of which son was feeding him, but finally believed Jacob was Esau. The rest of this section is about Jacob's deception and his relationship with Esau.

Rebekah's story is in some ways complex. She was complicit in the deception of her husband, she favored one son over the other. As a mother, it is hard to envision favoritism, but it does and did happen. We can probably label this family as a bit dysfunctional. No one really knows how the parent's favoritism affected both Jacob and Esau. There was deception of Isaac, who was old and vulnerable due to his blindness. Jacob, with Rebekah's assistance tricked and lied to Isaac. In the long run, is it possible that Rebekah knew that Jacob would be a better man lead the nation? Do not forget, that God told Rebekah during her pregnancy that the older son would serve the younger, meaning Jacob would be the leader. Was this really a hurtful deception or did Rebekah listen to God? In the end, Jacob, despite his flaws, was a mentor to the Israelites, and, in a way, the father of Israel. Rebekah may have, as a mother, and God-follower knew this. One can make the statement that her actions were necessary, not maybe morally right, but right in the end.

## Lessons learned from Rebekah:

1. **Favoritism of children is hurtful to the whole family-**Not only did Rebekah favor Jacob, but Isaac favored Esau. A child needs love from both parents (if available). Love from parents allows a child to be self-confident and to show love to others. Favoritism should never occur.

2. **Rebekah left her homeland and her family to follow Gods calling-**she served God! She did what she needed to do.

3. **Ask God for help-**God gave Rebekah two sons, but she did not ask God directly for His assistance, Isaac prayed on her behalf. Psalms121:2- "My help comes from the LORD, who made heaven and earth." Rebekah was given children but could have and should have gone to God herself.

4. **God has a plan-**God's plan was to have Jacob become the Hebrew patriarch-even though Rebekah was deceitful to her husband, God's plan prevailed. Would this have occurred naturally without, deceit? Good question. She heard God tell her, the older will serve the younger. Could this have been handled differently? It is not good to be deceitful, always be honest and forthright. This ended the way God wanted but could also have had disastrous results. She manipulated her husband—no matter what the outcome.

(24)

# Chapter 20

## Shiphrah and Puah-Exodus 1: 15-21

Even though Shiphrah and Puah have a small section in the Bible, they played an especially important role in the future of Israel. Shiphrah and Puah were Hebrew midwives. They were commanded by the king of Egypt or Pharaoh to kill all the male Hebrew babies. The story begins with Pharaoh becoming concerned about the number of Israelites. He told his people, "Look the Israelites have become far too numerous for us. Come, we must deal shrewdly with them or they will become even more numerous and, if war breaks out, will join our enemies, fight against us, and leave the country." The king of Egypt was afraid that because of the large numbers of them, the Israelites, would rise an overthrow him and his dynasty. Then the king said to Shiphrah and Puah, "When you are helping the Hebrew women during childbirth on the delivery stool, if you see the baby is a boy, kill him; but if it is a girl, let her live." The midwives feared God and did not do what the king mandated.

The king of Egypt continued to see male children being born to the Israelites. He summoned the midwives, Shiphrah and Puah and asked them, "Why have you done this? Why have you let the boys live?" They answered him, "Hebrew women are not like Egyptian women; they are vigorous and give birth before the midwives arrive." God blessed the midwives by giving them families of their own, while the Israelites became even more numerous.

This is another story of brave women, who feared God. The Bible does not designate Shiphrah and Puah as Israelites, but as Hebrew midwives, whose role was to assist the Israelite women as the give birth. Probably, they were not Israelites, which makes their role in the future of Israel most important. They disobeyed an edict from the Pharaoh to kill male babies of the Israelites. Their refusal could have meant certain punishment for them, but they believed in God and would not take part in any killing. The Israelites expanded and Shiphrah and Puah had families of their own.

## Lessons learned from Shiphrah and Puah:

1. **We must obey God, not man**-People make all kinds of excuses, not adhere to God's teachings. Shiphrah and Puah could have killed male Hebrew children as they were mandated to, but they feared God and did the right thing. They may have risked their lives, but again they were not going to go against God.
2. **Godly women will protect life**-It is important that all life is valued. Shiphrah and Puah were not protecting their own children's lives, but the lives of children that will never be a part of their lives, yet they knew the importance of life for everyone.
3. **Anyone's actions can benefit generations of people**-what Shiphrah and Puah did affects the Israelites even now. If they had adhered to Pharaoh's edict, the Israelite people may not have even survived. We need to teach or children, grandchildren, family, friends, co-workers, etc. about believing in God. When we believe, God will bless us many times over.

4. **When we put God in our lives, He will bless us-**like Shiphrah and Puah, who were blessed by God for doing the right thing, we too will be blessed. God is our Protector. When we believe in Him, we will be cared for. Our needs will be met.

5. **Every one of us is a person-**Shiphrah and Puah knew that the Hebrew mothers giving both were human beings, as was their babies. They respected life. We need to remember that every one of us was created by God. We need to treat each other with respect and dignity.

(25)

# Chapter 21

## Tamar-Genesis-38

The story of Tamar is one of loss, deceit, and tenacity. The story of Tamar begins with Judah. Judah married a Canaanite woman and had a son by her. The son's name was Er. The woman conceived again and had another son, named Onan. Later she gave birth to a third son named Shelah. Judah got a wife for Er. Her name was Tamar. But Er was wicked in the LORD's sight, so God put him to death. Judah then told Onan, "Sleep with your brother's wife and fulfill your duty to her as a brother-in-law to raise up offspring for your brother." However, Onan knew if he impregnated Tamar and she had a child, then he would lose his inheritance as the oldest son because the child even though would not be biologically Er's, would be raised as if it were Er's. Plus, Onan knew the child would not be his biological child. Onan did sleep with Tamar but spilled his semen on the ground to keep from providing offspring for his brother. What he did was wicked to the LORD, so the LORD put him to death also.

Judah probably at this point had some regrets about Tamar marrying his youngest son, Shelah, but he told her, "Live as a widow in your father's household until my son Shelah grows up." Judah sent Tamar back to her family. I believe probably at this point he wanted her as far away from his family as possible.

After a long time, Judah's wife died. After Judah mourned the death of his wife, he went up to Timnah, to the men who were shearing his sheep. Tamar by now was told that Judah was on his way to shear his sheep.

She then devised a plan. She took off her widow's clothes, covered herself with a veil to disguise herself and then sat down at the entrance to Enaim, which is on the road to Timnah. Tamar realized that Shelah had grown up, but Judah did not give him to Tamar for her to be his wife. When Judah saw her, he thought she was a prostitute. He did not recognize her because her face was covered. Not knowing that she was his daughter-in-law, Judah went over to her and said, "Come now, let me sleep with you." Tamar knew this man was Judah. She had a plan all along to get pregnant by him. She said to Judah, "And what will you give me to sleep with you?" Judah told her that he would send her a goat from his flock. Tamar replied, "Will you give me something as a pledge until you send it?" Judah asked her what she would want as a pledge. She replied. "Your seal and its cord, and the staff in your hand." Judah agreed and gave her the seal, its cord, and the staff. He then slept with her. After she left Judah, she took off her widow's clothes. Of course, Tamar became pregnant.

Meanwhile, Judah's friend took the goat to Tamar so that the pledge can fulfilled, as well as returning Judah's seal, cord, and staff to him. The friend was unable to find Tamar. Judah's friend asked the men in the town if anyone knew the shrine prostitute who was beside the road at Enaim. The men informed Judah's friend that there has not been any shrine prostitute in the area. Judah's friend went back to Judah and told him that, "I didn't find her. Besides, the men who lived there said, 'There hasn't been any shrine prostitute here.'" Judah was probably very confused. He told his friend to let Tamar keep the seal, cord, and staff. "After all, Judah said, I did send her this young goat, but you didn't find her." Judah was also concerned that this entire incident would make him a laughingstock.

Three months later, Tamar was accused of prostitution due to her pregnancy. When Judah found out, he was angry. He said, "Bring her out and have her burned to death!" As she was being brought out to be burned, she sent a message to Judah. Tamar said, "I am pregnant by the man that owns these" (referring to the seal, cord, and staff). She then asked if Judah recognized the items that he gave her. Judah did recognize them and so released Tamar from the death sentence. Tamar gave birth to twin boys, Perez and Zerah.

The story of Tamar is complex. Both her husbands died by the hand of God. Judah promised her to his third son but broke that promise. She devised a plan and became pregnant by Judah. Did she "use" Judah because she was angry? If she had married Shelah, one would suspect that she would be quite a few years older than him. Would that union even have been possible? One thing for Tamar, she was a tenacious woman, who in the end remained forever tied to Judah.

## Lessons learned from Tamar:

1. **Tamar was a victim**-both her husbands were wicked and died by God's hand. She was lied to by her father-in-law. She did persevere. Maybe not in the right way, but she hung in there. Lying and tricking people can have negative consequences. I would say Tamar was saved due to her twins, especially Perez. Perez is in the genealogy of King David.
2. **God had a plan**-Tamar survived and had offspring. Perez had a role in the Israelite nation.

# Chapter 22

## The Widow at Zarephath-1 Kings 17:7-24

Although nameless, this woman is important enough to be mentioned in my book. As with other women, her story is intertwined with that of Elijah, but I want this chapter to focus on her. The story with her begins in Zarepath. Zarepath has had no rain. God told Elijah, "Go at once to Zarepath in the region of Sidon and stay there. I have directed a widow there to supply you with food." When Elijah arrived in Zarepath, he saw the widow gathering sticks. He called to her and asked her to bring him some water so he may have a drink. As she was going to get the water, Elijah asked her to also bring him some bread. She told Elijah, "As surely as the LORD, your God lives, I don't have any bread-only a handful of flour in a jar and a little olive oil in a jug. I am gathering a few sticks to take home and make a meal for myself and my son, that we may eat it and die." This woman was obviously in dire straits regarding food and water. In her mind, this was probably the last meal that she and her son would have. Elijah told her not to be afraid, but to make her meal for her and her son. He added that she should make a small loaf of bread for him (Elijah) and then make something for herself and her son. He told her that God said, "the jug of flour will not be used up and the jug of oil will not run dry until the day the LORD sends rain on the land." In other words, God will take care of her!

The woman went away and did as Elijah instructed her to do. There was food every day for Elijah and for the woman and her family. The jug of flour was not used up and the jug of olive oil did not run dry.

Sometime later, the son of the woman became ill. He was so sick that he stopped breathing. The woman said to Elijah, "What do you have against me, man of God? Did you come to remind me of my sin and kill my son?" Elijah ended up bringing, through God, the child back to life. The widow told Elijah that she believed he is man of God.

## Lessons learned from the Widow at Zarepath:

1. **Never give up**-even when times are desperate, God id in control. In this case He sent Elijah to strengthen her belief in God.
2. **Do not be discouraged**-God is working for us! We may not see it immediately, but He is there for us. He has a plan for our lives.
3. **Help others**-this woman barely had food to eat, but she did what Elijah told her to do. It is important to help those in need. Even if could just give a little to those who are worse off than we are, God knows what we have done.

# Chapter 23

## Zipporah-Exodus 2: 18-22, 4:19-26, 18: 1-6

The story of Zipporah begins with Moses fleeing to Midian after killing an Egyptian who was beating a Hebrew. Because of the killing, Pharaoh wanted to kill Moses. This, Moses fled Egypt to Midian. One day he was sitting by a well when he noticed Jethro's (a priest of Midian), daughters drawing water from the well to water their father's flocks. Other shepherds came along and tried to drive the women away from the well, but Moses intervened, drove the shepherds away and watered their flocks. When his daughters told their father, Reuel, what happened at the well, he invited Moses to eat with the family. Moses ends up staying with Jethro. Jethro gives his daughter, Zipporah to Moses in marriage. Moses and Zipporah have a family.

After God told Moses to go back to Egypt, he took his wife and sons, put them on a donkey and started back to Egypt. At a lodging place on the way the LORD met Moses. He came to kill him. One theory for God's wanting to kill Moses is because his son was not circumcised since Zipporah did not approve of it. But Zipporah took a flint knife, cut off her son's foreskin and touched Moses' feet with it. Zipporah then said, "Surely you are a bridegroom of blood (circumcision) to me." So, the LORD left him alone. It is unsure of what Zipporah meant when she spoke this sentence, but she saved Moses and he went on to lead the Hebrews out of slavery. (26)

Zipporah did play an important role in the future of the Hebrew people. She was not a Hebrew woman but was a Midian. She did not share the same beliefs as Moses did. She did not believe in circumcision Moses, compromised by not having their second son, Eliezer circumcised. More than likely, this the reason God was incensed with Moses, because he did keep the covenant of circumcision. But in the end, Zipporah, kept the covenant, saved Moses, who saved the Hebrew nation.

Zipporah and Moses were married for 40 years, though it may not have been a typical marriage. Sometime before the actual Exodus, Moses sent her and the two boys back to her father. When Jethro went back to visit Moses in the wilderness, he brought back Zipporah and their sons. After this section, Zipporah is not mentioned again. Her legacy is one of controversy. She more than likely was at odds with Moses over his beliefs, which were so different from hers, yet she saves her husband from death by circumcising their son, an action which she was opposed to. She probably encouraged Moses to forego some of his beliefs. I would like to think of her as caring about her husband and honoring his covenant with God.

## Lessons learned from Zipporah:

1. **Honor God's law**-it is easy to stray from God's laws. That is a choice. We need to honor, respect and trust God, always.
2. **Know when you are not in fellowship with God-** ask forgiveness and repent.

3. **God can use anyone for anything-**in this case, He used a Midian, woman who was quick-thinking to save Moses.
4. **Forgiveness from God is quick-**we need to recognize what we did wrong, rectify it and ask forgiveness.

(27)

# Summary

Every woman in the Hebrew Bible should be a lesson to women of all religions. There are a few common themes that are attributed to all these women, even the "bad girls":

1. **Trust in God, always-**He loves us and will take care of us.
2. **Do what is right and stand up for God-**This is so relevant know with all the strife not only in our country, but around the world as well. If we stand up for God, adhere to His teachings, then we are showing others, that God will take care of us.
3. **Do good deeds-**God knows what we do and what is in our hearts. Something as simple as holding a door open for someone, giving someone else a parking spot that you might have wanted, letting someone who is behind you check out ahead of you or even just a smile or a kind word. It is the seemingly little things that we do that can make a difference in someone's life.
4. **God's plan & God's timing-**In God's time, not ours. We want what we want, and we want it now. That may not be God's plan. He will give us what we need on his time.
5. **Be thankful for what we have-**do not be jealous, greedy, or prideful. Those are not qualities that embody Godly women.
6. **Be careful with the words we speak-**what we say and how we say it can build someone up or tear someone down.

7. **Praise God-**we need to praise God many times during the day. Be grateful that he gave us another day.
8. **There is a Day of Judgement-**We will be judged on how good or bad we have been. Did we do good deeds? Did we help people in need? Behave well and obey God's rules. This will determine our destiny in the afterlife.
9. **God can use anyone-** We need to ask ourselves, "What does God want from me today?" When bad things happen, we need to learn from them. Talk to God, read the Bible. He will give us understanding.
10. **Be humble, not prideful-**It is important that we are not self-serving. We need to give God credit; not ourselves. When we do a good deed, we are doing it for the good of the person or people we are helping, not for our own gain.

**Deuteronomy 31:8- "The Lord himself goes before you and will be with you; he will never leave you or forsake you. Do not be afraid; do not be discouraged."**

There are many books and articles on woman of the Hebrew Bible available. Mine is one of many that will hopefully inspire women to live a good life, adhering to God's rules.

# References


1. ibelieve.com. Abigail in the Bible: "5 Things All Women Can Learn from Her". By Debbie McDaniel, June 12, 2019
2. Recognize and Remember: Recognizing, Recording and Remembering God's faithfulness. "Lessons learned from Bathsheba's life (especially in her mothering)". By Sandrajo, May 27, 2009
3. The Eagle. "Finding lessons in tale of Lot's daughters." By Peter Tarlow Jun 2, 2018
4. Rosevinecottagegirls.com. 'Powerful Lessons From Deborah In The Bible." By Rosevine Cottage Girls, July 27, 2020
5. The Diligent Woman: Walking Confidently in God's Words. "Lessons from Dinah, Tamar, and Tamar the daughter of David." Accessed October 26, 2020
6. Time Tracts: Redeeming the time, because the day are evil. Ephesians 5:16. "The Story of Dinah." Accessed October 26, 2020
7. Womenofnotablecharacter.com. "9 Impactful Lessons We Can Learn from the Book of Esther in the Bible."
8. The Diligent Woman: Walking Confidently in God's Word. "Lessons from Eve." Accessed October 26, 2020
9. Out Upon the Waters: Stories and Resources for Stepping Out in Faith. "6 Life Lessons We Learn from Eve." Posted by Rebecca, Jun 25, 2018
10. Farirai Baya. "5 Things I Learned from Hagar's Encounter With God." Farirai Baya, June 9, 2019
11. Joyful Abundant Life: Finding Joy In Any Season. "5 Significant lessons from the life of Hannah." Accessed October 27, 2020

12. Biblestudytools. Com. "Powerful Lessons from the Unusual Story of Jael." By Jenna Martin, July 5, 2019

13. Letterpile." Jezebel and the Lessons We Learn From Her." By Margaret Minnicks, August 18, 2019

14. Faraboverubiescollection.com. "Lessons From Jochebed On How To Balance the Risks and Rewards Involved in Making Our Dreams a Reality." By Nina Dafe, Accessed October 29, 2020

15. "Rachel And Leah: Three Lessons Leah Can Teach Us About Beauty and Body Image." By Heather Creekmore. Accessed November 6, 2020

16. Women of Noble Character. "Lessons We Can Learn From Miriam in the Bible." Access on November 19, 2020.

17. The Basilica. "Ruth and Naomi: A Story of Redemption." June 14, 2020

18. Tikvat Israel Congregation. "Why Did Rachel Steal Laban's Household Idols? "Accessed December 17, 2020

19. Women's Bible Study. "Why did Rachel steal the idols, conclusion." March 24, 2016

20. The Diligent Woman. "Lessons from Rachel." Accessed December 17, 2020

21. Womenofnoblecharacter.com "Rachel in the Bible: Lessons from a Love Story." Accessed December 17, 2020

22. One for Israel. "THE SECRETS OF RAHAB'S ROPE." June 10, 2018

23. Diligent Woman. "Lessons from Rahab." Accessed December 18, 2020

24. Rememberandrecognize.com. "Lessons Learned From Rebekah." Accessed December 21st, 2020

25. Teaching Help: The Writings of Kim Higginbotham. "Shiphrah & Puah-Lessons from Courageous Women." June 5, 2019

26. Biblegateway.com. "ZIPPORAH: The Woman Who Wrongly Opposed Her Husband." Accessed December 23, 2020

27. The Diligent Woman. "Quick Action: Lessons from Zipporah." Accessed December 23, 2020